The Becoming Woman
Transitioning from the season of waiting to intentionally courting

Esther Jacob

Foreword by Keeley Stephenson
Contribution by Audrey Chamunorwa

The Becoming Woman

Women!

Women are valuable gifts and treasures from above. Women are powerful; women are special; women are precious; women are worth much more.

Charm is deceitful and beauty is vain, but a woman who fears the Lord is to be praised. Give her of the fruit of her hands and let her works praise her in the gates."

Proverbs 31:30-31.

The Becoming Woman

THE BECOMING WOMAN
Transitioning from the season of waiting to intentionally courting.

Copyright © 2023 by Esther Jacob.

All rights reserved. No portion of this book without permission may be reproduced, stored in a retrieval system, or transmitted in any form – scanned, electronic, photocopied or recorded without written consent of the author as it is strictly prohibited. Excerpts and links may be used, provided that full and clear credit is given to the author with specific direction and reference to the original content.

If you would like to use material from the book for short quotations or occasional page copying for personal or group study, this is permitted other than for review purposes. However, prior written permission must be obtained on request by emailing the author on info@authenticworth.com. All that's written in the book is solely the author's journey and experiences which can be used as quotes referenced clearly.

Unless otherwise indicated, scripture quotations are taken from the New International Version (NIV), the Message Version (MSG) and the Easy Standard Version (ESV).

Paperback ISBN: 978-1-7396607-1-0
Hardback ISBN: 978-1-7396607-2-7
e-book ISBN: 978-1-7396607-3-4

Publisher: Authentic Worth
Website: www.authenticworth.com

Authentic Worth Publishing is bringing worth back into you through storytelling and book writing!

The Becoming Woman

Dedicated to The Becoming Woman; as you read and study this book, our aim is to provide a range of inspiring, authentic and relatable moments shared with the author.

In addition, we have 7 books published for your consideration:

It's Time to Heal – *A woman's journey to self-discovery and freedom.*

Completion – *From the perspective of brokenness.*

From Glory to Glory – *Great beauty in seasons of pain; Strong at the broken places.*

The Power of a Forward-Thinking Mindset – *Breaking strongholds in the mind.*

Confident Face – *Embracing your authentic beauty.*

Abundant Progress – *Maximising the gradual steps of the journey.*

The Becoming Woman – *Transitioning from the season of waiting to intentionally courting.*

Signed copies: www.authenticworth.com/books

The Becoming Woman

Acknowledgements

Writing isn't a hobby; it's not something to take up space or make time go quickly. It is purpose-led and transformational in many people's lives locally and globally. To embrace the journey of writing and allow the words to flow from the mind and transferring them on paper is the reason I press on for the current and upcoming generation, to be obedient to the calling on my life and make influential impact. Making a name is great, but changing the life of one person is an expensive investment they will remember for the rest of their days on earth.

Words change lives when used wisely and for this reason, I want to take this opportunity to thank Almighty God for constantly downloading visions, dreams and ideas to write meaningful books; this being the 7th. The Becoming Woman is dedicated to young girls, teenagers, youths, adults, mothers and women around the world who've experienced and currently going through seasons of waiting in various forms. I am not only thankful for the opportunity to share my story, but to see the number of lives being changed one step at a time.

I also want to thank my family – my amazing parents, Mr and Mrs Jacob, my siblings – The Late Glory Jacob (who would be honoured to not only witness this book, but stepping into the new season I'm in), my sister, Ruth and brother, Faith, my fiancé, friends, sisters, brothers, clients, and the wider community for their constant support and encouragement throughout the journey of writing this book. I don't usually announce when a new book is in the process of being published, but through life's experiences, intimate talks and transparency with loved ones, my passion is continually stirred from there to continue being an inspiration to the world. Their attentiveness in praying, interceding, listening, and transparent tears have kept me going.

Having written and published my first book in 2016, I knew that one book wasn't enough and for that reason, I pursued the journey of writing not as a hobby, but a calling to purpose and creativity for other books to be birthed. As a multi-published author, I choose to surround myself with like-minded people because in the multitude of counsel, there is safety. Throughout my journey of writing, each

The Becoming Woman

book has its own unique beginning and end, and what makes it special is the community I have around me to continue on the journey. Being grounded and focused in the right environment enables me to serve and write more books now and for the future.

I don't want you to assume this is an easy task; writing a book takes strength and focus because as a writer, you are pouring out and making an intentional decision to serve the masses. It takes resilience and tenacity to keep going, even when you don't know when a breakthrough will occur. You just know that the investment will be worth it and you will see the fruits in due course.

To The Becoming Woman; thank you for taking the time to stop by and read this book. I've written it as an addition to your journey to personal growth and development; a reminder to remember how valuable you are. This book is dedicated to the singles, women in the courting season, fiancées and wives to be; not to forget our local and global sisters for the support in your fellow sister's journey of growth! You are all special and cherished very much! Thank you for holding your sister's hand on the journey. I promise you; it will be a great one to cherish! Let's get started…

The Becoming Woman

Contents Page

Foreword by Keeley Stephenson	1
Contribution by Audrey Chamunorwa	2
Introduction	4
Chapter O.N.E. The Becoming Woman	9
Chapter T.W.O. Can you Endure being Single?	19
Chapter T.H.R.E.E. Take a Break	31
Chapter F.O.U.R. Unbroken	42
Chapter F.I.V.E. The Courting Process	52
Chapter S.I.X. Money and Savings	66
Chapter S.E.V.E.N. Love or Lust	75
Chapter E.I.G.H.T. The Becoming Gentleman	85
Chapter N.I.N.E. Enjoy your Life	99
Chapter T.E.N. Own your Season	108
10 Truths The Becoming Woman Needs to Know	115
Notes	121

The Becoming Woman

Foreword by Keeley Stephenson

To the Esther I knew when she was single. It was amazing to witness your heart's posture and faith. Although some aspects of the journey were difficult, you persevered and kept believing like the Queen you were and still are.

This gives someone like me hope and will definitely stir the faith in others to not give up when it comes to receiving God's best for them. This also proves that there truly is power in prayer and that God hears us even when we think He isn't listening. Thank you for not settling and choosing to wait.

To the Esther that is now a Fiancé. Man, I am so proud of you! To see your journey from the beginning and watch you bask, enjoy and delight in God's gift to you is also a gift to me.

Love looks so good on you and it's such a joy to watch you glow and live out one of your hearts desires that God made come true for you. I absolutely adore this for you and it's such an honour to bear witness to this season of your life.

To the Esther that will soon marry, if there's anyone I could say has what it takes to be an excellent wife, it's you! The way you nurture, care and tend to others is truly beautiful. You really do carry the Proverbs 31 Woman with grace and anointing, and I look forward to seeing you step into wifehood.

I also look forward to seeing how this beautiful new journey moulds and shapes you and how you and your Fiancé take hold of your unified destinies to carry out great exploits together.

Thank you for allowing me to be a part of your journey and thank you both for not giving up until you found each other.

The Becoming Woman

Contribution by Audrey Chamunorwa

"And let us not grow weary in doing good, for in due season we will reap if we do not give up."

Galatians 6:9.

Waiting, waiting well...

It's never easy having to wait for someone or something, especially when we desire and see so much beauty in it. The longer the wait seems, the further away obtaining it feels.

"Surely, if it's meant for me, I shouldn't have to wait this long!"

This becomes a back-and-forth battle in our minds in the midst of waiting. So truly, what benefit does waiting aid to us? As frustrating as it can be, I've found it to be an instrument which plays chords of success. The melodious space to evaluate, prepare and build the tenacity required to reach for the things we desire. Waiting is the machinery used to exercise patience, the process of becoming and the dosage of humility we need.

Being of close proximity to Esther, I was humbled and privileged to watch her journey of waiting. In this case, waiting for her life partner. As the scripture above states, through the times when the dating scene looked dry, unpromising and discouraging, Esther remained true to herself. What she desired, she did not compromise. She actively prayed, availed herself to being in a space to serve, grow and become the woman who was ready for what she was waiting for.

A lot of times we find ourselves only asking, yet not preparing ourselves to be in better positions to receive what we are yearning for. In a world of desperation and taking whatever comes our way,

The Becoming Woman

Esther remained poised and focused by living righteously and being surrounded with the right people which was integral to her. She became open, hopeful that what she was praying for in due time will come to pass and IT DID!

This is my encouragement to you that as you wait, allow yourself to become the candidate for what you're hoping for. As you wait, assess your environment, what you feed your mind with and the people you surround yourself with; do they encourage the growth that is taking place in your life?

Finally, as you wait, don't get tired of doing what is good, for in due time you will surely harvest the fruits of good waiting!

The Becoming Woman

Introduction

A woman who is becoming opens her mouth with wisdom and kindness. She is not influenced easily by the opinions of others because she constantly takes the time to invest in herself. She isn't selfish in doing this; she is mindful and focused on her growth. Working on herself is the highest goal. Yes, she is aware of her flaws; some obvious than others, but she uses them to the best of her ability, turning them into strengths and helping other women do the same.

The woman you are currently sitting next to or the sister you visit from time to time is going through secret battles and insecurities that've impacted them from tender ages; from physical appearance insecurities due to society's standards of 'beauty', feeling left out, domestic violence, unaccomplished goals unmet, the waiting season, and other contributing factors. Some women who won't take the time to understand who they are or aren't fully aware of what they've been assigned to will be swayed to entertain thoughts of their beauty being dependent on the adorning of pearls or the extensive splashing of money spent, but none of these matter in the eyes of the becoming woman who makes a decision to work on herself internally.

There is more emphasis on a woman defined by a gentle and quiet character; her eloquent but few words. To the woman who speaks less and works smart; I salute you. When a woman loses her character, she loses credibility, humility, integrity and the influence of others which eventually attracts the wrong attention. Her influence should be on having an impact with the wider community before she can represent other women in her immediate circle.

She is relatable to others and understands that when she walks in a room, the atmosphere already changes because she isn't there to blend in with the crowd. She creates a powerful legacy by her words, actions and deeds. In order to do this, she must learn how to embrace seasons of seclusion without the interruption of others. She values time and needs to regain focus in seasons of solitude.

What attracts a good man to a woman isn't just her appearance, but the influential charisma she has towards him. There is a unique gift that a woman carries within herself and portrays it in a way that

The Becoming Woman

isn't desperate or needy. This is also known as quiet time with self. A quality man *knows* what he is looking for in a woman. A quality woman *knows* what she desires in a man. Notwithstanding, the becoming woman is content in enjoying her season until the appointed time when she is ready to be found. She isn't trying to be noticed or create noise just to impress the opposite sex. She knows that less is more when communicating and listening attentively because she only has time to go where she's aligned to.

The becoming woman is capable of managing her changing seasons which impacts how others see her when the storms rage. She is quick to listen and absorb information; she is mindful about what is being released in her thoughts. She knows who she is assigned to and refuses to spread herself too thin. In turn, she is able to manage her emotions effectively to avoid breaking down. It is healthy to release the tears and frustrations to start again. Be willing to start from scratch if you have to and set yourself free. Breathe in; breathe out…

She knows that the increase on influence includes an increase on her vulnerability. *The more vulnerable; the more powerful*, which is important to take note of this: "Some women can't go where you are heading to because they refuse to grow." What do I mean by this? I am referring to developing in maturity, transparency, and an honest conversation with self. Vulnerability costs, but it will pay off in the long run when done in the right way and at the right time.

> **The Becoming Woman knows when it's time to let go and keep moving forwards.**

In addition, it is a vital necessity to let go and forgive. In order for the becoming woman to have increased territory, authority and bear abundant fruit in her season, she must operate in the realm of letting go of grudges and bitterness to embrace the warmth of forgiveness and freedom. This is her power as she takes control and works on her emotional intelligence and wellbeing. The more she walks in freedom, dignity and purpose, the better she is in *becoming*. She is first of all, **IN-fluenced** by her own journey as she takes a glimpse

The Becoming Woman

at the moments that made her who she currently is and positions herself as an advocate for others to learn from.

She discerns when something is off and starts with herself rather than looking at the external and find someone else to blame. She is responsible and leaves room for people to grow, whilst remembering that *she is enough*. The becoming woman knows that at the right time, she will be celebrated, but rather than waiting for others to salute her, she finds praise and approval in the One who made her beautifully and perfectly.

Women are created uniquely. Women realise that every day is a process despite the good and bad battling each other at the same time. She prepares her day in advance to inspire future queens, mothers, teachers, advocates etc. She knows that it isn't possible doing life alone, so she is mindful that the more weight being given to her, the more her tolerance threshold will increase to the level of her influence. The more pressure exposed to her equates to more power being able to handle it. Through it all, she is aware that what her mind focuses on will grow.

> **Her relationship with daily development is her most precious asset.**

The becoming woman is known to be virtuous. When a woman hides herself in God's Presence, the man ordained for her should apply Matthew 6:33. She doesn't expose herself to every man that offers a compliment because her discernment levels are active each moment of the day. God is not looking for a perfect woman; He is looking for an imperfect woman who knows she is broken and needs refreshing.

Proverbs 31 describes the qualities of a good wife and is a key favourite among women who are trusting in the transition of waiting to courting, leading to Godly marriage. The good wife exalts and is trusted by her husband, adored by her children, works exceedingly well to take care of the household and even makes her own clothing!

The Becoming Woman

She taps into the goodness of God as He enables her paths to drip with abundance in reference to Psalm 65:11. She is a lender and not a borrower. The becoming woman is strong, not needing anyone to be liable on but God. She always confides in Him through her struggles by going to the Throne. As women continue to discover who they are, let's remember that we too, are growing daily, being able to support other women in their transformative seasons.

Be mindful of other women in seasons who are broken and need time away from their environments. It has nothing to do with you for the moment, so be careful not to take offence when there is silence; perhaps they have lost confidence in who they are; their friends may have betrayed them, or going through family disagreements or dysfunctions.

> **You don't have to always be in a woman's face, but you have to *respect* her space.**

We'll be in at much peace when we admit our faults to one another including the slip-ups, weaknesses and wrongs. As iron sharpens iron, so does a friend sharpen another friend to be corrected in firm love (Proverbs 27:17 – emphasis added). When a woman senses in her heart that another woman is out of place, the becoming woman sacrifices quality time to support her mentally and emotionally. Eventually, they both become stronger and able to help each other overcome past traumas.

Unspoken troubles may have ensnared the becoming woman, but she is ready to overcome them by reaching out to her sister in confident trust. At some point in our lives, we must learn to identify who our confidantes are, and transparently be open with them on where we are in life. Some women struggle with past relationships, friendships, hurts, and secret battles that won't ever go away until you give her permission to be herself and speak. Women are designed to help each other. They are meant to offer encouragement and motivation to be better than yesterday and prepare them for tomorrow.

The Becoming Woman

Time is a precious commodity and shouldn't be spent on analysing another woman's journey. We don't own tomorrow, let alone our lives, so refuse to add more problems to someone else's journey of development. Jealousy and envy arise, but you have the authority to stop them from occurring.

When you see your sister rejoicing and celebrating their small and big wins, join in and be happy for her. No one said it was easy, and even though women are talented and skilled at making it look easy, apply wisdom to ask her questions and give her time to respond when she is ready to do so. If you've built the right genuine relationships, you've definitely won a sister or two who you can share your story with.

Remember that some of your ordained sisters have several assignments in your life; some for a length of time and others for a season; regardless, learn to embrace them when they come and when they go.

The becoming woman will encounter various trials and tribulations and their *patience will be tested*. There will be closed doors. This is not uncommon. Rejection is for your own protection, and when you remember this, you'll realise the excess love that God has for you because He is constantly protecting and preparing you for greater. Despite all she goes through, the becoming woman chooses to learn from life's experiences and uses them to shape her personal journey to leave a lasting legacy of perseverance.

Continue reading on; take notes, meditate, pause for a while, let the words sink in, and let's dive into learning about the expensive value of transitioning from the season of waiting to intentionally courting.

Remember that in the process of becoming, you are constantly learning. I am excited for you and look forward to seeing your life transform. Your new beginning starts today!

Chapter O.N.E.
-
The Becoming Woman

"Even though you see me at face value, it doesn't mean I didn't have to pay a price to get here."

Woman! Womb-man – a woman treasured in her mother's womb before her existence came into the world. She came because her value matters; she will inspire and change the world one step at a time. It all started with a thought that became an idea; that idea became a reality and birthed multiple seeds of powerful, intentional women with a goal to uplift, transform and shake nations. A woman holds great strength and tenacity whether she realises it or not. She may not be exposed to who she is right now, but she is definitely on the cusp of it. She's constantly in a season of change, aware that it won't always be comfortable; nonetheless, she is ready for the challenge to make her stronger.

> **I see the Becoming Woman as an individual running her own race.**

The becoming woman isn't attached to her past failures, but uses them to bring her one step closer to Destiny. Let's be transparent: it's okay to be concerned about certain moments where your life doesn't match up to your expectations or what you had in mind. Even in your current situation, there will be seasons of uncertainty because you won't always see what's on the other side. This is part of the growth process because knowing everything at once is a hefty task. No matter the season, the beauty is in being still – note; this isn't to be confused with stagnation. Being still is an opportunity to ponder, reflect and meditate on the journey, whilst stagnation is

The Becoming Woman

simply agreeing with where you currently are – no aim to move forwards for fear of failing – this is not your portion!

No one knows the future the way God does, and this is why it gives us the opportunity to trust Him with our lives. I've experienced known and unknown seasons where I've had no choice but to look up, reassuring myself that I am always guided. We don't have what it takes to be the author of own lives without the intervention of the Divine.

*"But Esther, it's easy for you to say that, however, God is taking **too long!** How long do I have to wait?"*

***Answer**: "You have to rest and let God stand; if you take matters into your own hands, you will delay the process."*

You will appreciate the beauty of delayed gratification when you change your perspective. Until your perspective changes, you will always see and have what you say. The waiting season is preparing you for what you're asking for, and this includes building your character to be in alignment with where God is taking you.

When you are in the season of waiting, the woman is becoming.

When you are becoming, it doesn't require you to disturb her. She needs space to grow and transform. Look at it this way; when you become the CEO of your own company and take matters into your own hands, or you refuse to share the vision with someone other than yourself, it will become difficult to handle. All roads can't lead to you as the CEO – be confident to delegate and expand the vision as you build collectively with others. We know that God is the overseer of what we do, and when we place our desires into His Hands, we are able to use time wisely and work smarter. This includes knowing when to rest and when to take action.

The Becoming Woman

In quiet seasons, we learn how God works. I am confident that even when I don't see or feel anything happening, God never stops working. At times, our environments and what we see may tell you to take the quicker route, but the challenge for us is to work on trusting God's timing. God shows us how awesome He is every day. If not for Him on our side waking us from our beds and being able to go about our duties is a blessing that shouldn't be underrated. Underestimating the Great One and who you are will hold you back from what is expected to come your way.

No matter how many friends are surrounded by you, the call of temptation may entice you to give up and cut corners. Analysing your circle is vital and being able to write down a list of those who need you and those who feed you is a daily process because people and life change. There is beauty in being open with others whilst having healthy boundaries at the same time.

For the woman who is seeking a higher purpose to life and understanding who she's been called to be takes private work. From a relationship perspective, this can be applied when it comes to *courting* (which we will expand on in chapter 5), especially when we're excited once a man shows interest in us. It's easy to 'do the most', making it quite uncomfortable for the man to discern whether this is the ideal woman.

As a becoming woman, it is important that you have healthy boundaries when getting to know a man and give him space. Your own privacy should be for you to focus on the areas that's causing you to be out of alignment, especially when you are uncomfortable about the next stages or unsure where the relationship is heading. It requires the becoming woman to speak less and avoid the pressure from different voices preventing her from going in the right direction.

The people you are surrounded with can take you higher or keep you in the same place. When you sense that you aren't being challenged to grow, evolve or transform, be intentional about the company you keep for your own growth and be willing to make changes.

It's important to be focused and intentional on what you desire. It's easy to be fixated on the external attributes of a man that women forget we are a work-in-progress. Our desires for the opposite sex will fall in place when we work on ourselves. The greatest gift you can give yourself is love, tenderness, kindness and patience. Yes, we are surrounded by many situations beyond our control, however, we have the choice to go with our feelings, or trust God to take over and have His way.

During my single season, I'd enjoy the company of His Presence, even when it was difficult to express myself in words. I'd do it in tears to bring closure, peace and clarity that I wasn't forgotten, and at the appointed time, I'd be in the relationship He intended for me. I saw the single season as an opportunity to dig deeper into areas of my life where brokenness from past situations were merely distractions. I intentionally chose to ignore the analysis of categorising when I should be in a relationship, reminding myself that I wasn't late.

At times, you will feel hidden and forgotten, and it is not deliberate. There are seasons in your life where you have to embrace being by yourself and working on those deep areas that cause you to act beyond who you are. When something doesn't align effectively, it becomes a barrier to growth. Refusing to accept correction is a sign of pride which prevents you from becoming the woman you've been called to be.

People are always watching you; whether online, on social media, at networking events, on the streets, etc. You have to be intentional about how you carry yourself *always*. Anytime you worry or entertain limiting beliefs about yourself, your influence subtracts. Life isn't without its battles and storms, but there is always an opportunity to grow from strange seasons and keep perseverance active.

As the author of this book, I'm in different seasons of waiting and won't always know when the breakthrough will come, however, that is what makes life exciting when I don't always know every step. The absence of not being in a relationship didn't deplete me. Being confidently stable in my singleness was a blessing. You will find out more when you continue reading the book!

You are not defined as more exclusive or favourable because you are in a relationship, courting, engaged, or married. In order to embrace your season at the appointed time, wait until it's your turn; you must learn to embrace the beautiful season of being single within yourself.

The Becoming Woman

> **Your season of singleness should never affect your peace or mental wellbeing!**

The mental battles of being alone or not having anyone by your side to some, is worrying. I know women can talk about how difficult it has been being single. It may be familiar to get married at a young age; perhaps early 20s, however, if you are in your 30s, the pressure starts particularly when living with your parents. It seems to be a taboo in our generation because we are expected to know better by moving out early. Is that so? Let's look at the following scenarios:

- *"You're meant to be out of your parent's house by 21 and living an independent life!"*
- *"How much money are you making at your age? There are other people who are doing better than you!"*
- *"How can you be 35 and still live with your mum?!"*
- *"When will you get on the property ladder and become a homeowner yourself?"*
- *"How can the man you desire find you when all you do is stay at home?"*

Be careful of what and who you listen to and let into your life, especially when you are in seasons of transition. Don't let the opinions of others dictate what you should do or come up with solutions in your own strength. The pressure to be among the crowd and have the title or feel tempted to show off in front of critics isn't to be used against those we love. We should never allow anyone to place that amount of pressure on us.

To rush and settle down is cheating your own relationship with loving who you are in the current season. It's not healthy to cut corners and settle just to create 'peace in your environment' when you don't possess peace within. A relationship which is filled with peace of mind builds gradually. Everything doesn't always need to be in order or the way you expect, because that's what takes out the mystery of life. However, having mental, emotional and spiritual stability is what keeps us sane to enjoy the journey and be expectant for what is ours.

The Becoming Woman

Being envious of your sister's engagement ring gives you the opportunity to identify why your mind has gone that far. It becomes easier to look down on yourself because others around you are getting engaged and married, however, as a becoming woman, you must understand that before two people become one, they once had a story.

We won't always know what stories or situations happened in one's past, or not yet ready to talk about the challenges they've gone through in their relationships; therefore, mentally envying another person's joy when we haven't taken the time to know their story is unhealthy.

When we hear several prophecies that have been spoken in the years past, and another person receives a word in less than a year, don't doubt the length of time it takes to get your own. It will still come to fruition.

The becoming woman should never be influenced by what is around her, but take the time to understand what thoughts are holding her back. Our temporary moments shouldn't make us think or speak negatively over our situations assuming they won't change. When you crack an egg, it can't go back to the normal position, and this is why it's important to be careful what you let into your heart. Don't allow the lips of other people to define your worth or tell you who you are. Yes, they may be intimidated by the anointing within you, however, that should not make you change who you are or devalue what is in you and be swayed by the opinions of others.

> **Question: As a becoming woman, when will you start creating quality time with yourself?**

Alone-time is what you need to ignite your life. When you're drained and don't know what to do or the steps to take, be intentional about using the time wisely and make healthy decisions on how to improve. Quality time is a great strength and love language that we must maximise in our lives. When you are able to master this, it becomes swift to encourage other women around you and invest in

The Becoming Woman

their wellbeing. A woman who knows her strength is uplifting and inspires others to do the same which raises her influence.

It's a rare gift and treasure to have this kind of woman in your life, and when she comes, make sure you cherish her. Because she knows her priorities, she ensures that wholeness and completion must take place before entertaining anyone else.

A confident woman is very attractive, not only to her fellow sisters, but to the opposite sex. You will know when a woman is confident by what she talks about, who she is surrounded by and has no time to be on platforms and environments where it minimises her personal growth. As a woman who is constantly pursuing destiny, working within doesn't just become a chore, but a discovering lifestyle.

A woman who doesn't take offence or bring offence to others is a woman of freedom and peace of mind. It may not always be possible to avoid offence or be offended by someone's attitude, however, being your best self is what will help avoid these distractions. Offences take up unnecessary space in your mind and as a becoming woman, it is important to remember what to learn from these triggers and make decisions that suit your lifestyle and not what others want you to be.

When I look back over my life to see how far God brought me, it helps me to know that the shortcuts would've costed me in the future. The eagerness to make it to the top and not be able to manage the workload would have me humbled. Nobody likes to be disgraced, so we must do ourselves a favour and embrace each step of the way and refuse to fight the pain of waiting. The waiting season is built as we master the mindset of developing the becoming woman within. We are all constantly working on ourselves to be better, wiser, richer (not just in finances), but health and building genuine relationships.

As women, we are uniquely powerful in collective and individual ways; we can serve and support one another with our gifts, skills and talents to strengthen us and those that were once damaged. Depending on the mindset you have and the willingness to learn from others, it's important to take time to:

1) **Build your strength up** – This can include taking time off social media, practising the art of gratitude, looking at what

you already have and making it work. At times, it is easy to neglect this because of what we are trying to attain, but before you see the beauty in tomorrow, you must strengthen what remains today.

2) **Focus on what matters** – What are your mental priorities? Remember that what you focus on, you magnify, so whatever you choose to glean on, make sure it's adding value to your personal growth and development.

3) **Ask relevant questions where you fall short in certain areas** – One of the greatest contributions to improvements are asking questions that relate to your season. What can I do to become better or how can I learn from the mistakes of the past, rather than allowing it to impact the present?

4) **Surround yourself with those who are more experienced than you** – The beauty of growth is in assessing and learning from those who are more experienced in the field you want to get into. As a becoming woman, you blossom in the right environments. Remember that you are a seed that is waiting to grow and influence your surroundings. Make it worthwhile!

5) **Be around like-minded women who are doing what you desire and learn from their skillset** – Worth is expensive! Lean on your sister's journey to find out what keeps her tenacious! When you see a woman doing very well, applaud her; she has positioned herself to network, meet other people and is willing to take heed to what she hears. She identifies who is relevant and chooses those who are able to enhance her knowledge.

The becoming woman is for a lifetime filled with great moments and much more to discover with no-one being exempt from life's lessons. We can't always assume that hard moments will subside and never have an impact on ones' wellbeing with the differing seasons in a woman's life. It takes strength and resilience to be different. To keep putting a smile on your face, and yet showing up

The Becoming Woman

to work, running your business, being a stay-at-home mum, supporting your children with their homework, running errands; to name a few. It can be challenging; however, these are the rewards of becoming the woman who is ready to face the next level.

Sis, remember that you are a rich gift to the world. Refuse to cut yourself short and rush the process of becoming you. It's in the becoming stages that you find out who you're called to be, how to adapt, and ultimately, showing up as your best self. As a becoming woman, it will take moments of reflection, tears and honesty to stand face-to-face answering those tough questions that strengthen you in the long run.

The better you are at working on yourself in the early stages, the easier it becomes to manage your internal and external environments. Life's experiences can make you aware of your purpose; one way or the other regarding painful or silent seasons, they eventually express what was already in you, and that is grace and strength to carry on.

In the next chapter, I want you to pause and take the time to ponder on the theme – *'Can you Endure being Single?'* – A rich topic so be prepared! Before you begin reading chapter 2, what thoughts come to mind about singleness? Write them here:

_____

_____

_____

_____

_____

_____

_____

_____

The Becoming Woman

How did it go when writing your thoughts? You can either keep it to yourself or share it with a trusted sister. As long as you are able to own your single season and live purposefully, you are on the right track of progress and focus. Therefore, it is important that you take the time to build the becoming woman within because she is doing her best. As the becoming woman evolves, she learns to position herself by working on her weaknesses, eventually turning them into strengths.

The becoming woman refuses to be distracted because she's in a season of transition and knows her time is near. When you are determined to reach the next level, there has to be stamina to keep going and not forfeit the promise. No matter how difficult it is right now, remember that life changes and you are too. Embracing the difficult moments will prune and sharpen your character, enabling you to enjoy the process of becoming.

Look up and remember where your help comes from. There is hope for you sis, and you will make it. Keep putting one foot in front of the other. You've got this always!

Reflection: Don't rush the process because there are many people who will be blessed by your patience, obedience and resilience in waiting! *#TheBecomingWoman*.

The Becoming Woman

Chapter T.W.O.

-

Can you Endure being Single?

"Can any one of you by worrying add a single hour to your life?"

Matthew 6:27.

When you think of the word *single*, what comes to mind? Envision a woman in her early 20s or late 30s; how do you think she maintains a healthy level of peace in this fast-paced generation? By taking the time to analyse her environment and assess what isn't adding value to her growth. In the seasons and stages of our lives, we must be confident and comfortable in assessing our environments to see what is helping us grow or causing us to shrink. Don't stay in a comfortable environment if you are not seeing positive changes in your life.

As a becoming woman, you have to own the responsibility of protecting your peace. Perhaps you may be her; you may be the woman wondering what the single season is preparing you for, or why you're still single. What pressures have you been entertaining that's causing you to doubt the season you are in? Yes, I am sure you've heard it many times that waiting is the best season, and, may I say, it truly is.

When I was in the single season, I didn't realise how much God loved me enough to wait. A song which has kept me during my single season is Travis Greene called 'You Waited.' This is a deep intimate song about the love of God, and how He never gives up on those who are in the waiting season. Taking the words of the song as it's played, I want you as the becoming woman to process the word; *w.a.i.t*. When God has a blessing to give you, He will prepare you by ensuring you are ready to handle what you've asked for. Your foundation of singleness is very important as that will keep you standing firm, so honour and feed it with words of affirmation and declaration.

The Becoming Woman

God will keep you in the waiting season to prune and bring out the best in you. Being single is about wholeness and wellness in every aspect of your life, and how you come across towards others (not to be taken lightly!). How you speak in your single season will indicate whether you are ready to be in a relationship. How you treat your family, friends and loved ones is indicative of being ready to pursue the next level.

Remember, being in a relationship is not just about two people, but a healthy community. Healthy conversations are birthed in environments where you can be yourself and appreciate others. Not trying to manipulate or jump ahead of yourself, but taking the time to listen when constructive criticism comes in conversations.

Singleness is attractive because you are fully confident in who you are without the attachment of being needy towards another person. No matter what season you're in, you will eventually see that your neediness to be with someone could be causing the delay. Whatever you need is already yours and it will come at the right time.

Doubt is real, but so is faith and prayer too. You have a choice to make by ensuring that in the slowest seasons of growth, you are able to understand that it is not a permanent state. What helps in particular is when you are able to relate and sympathise with women who need further encouragement and the reminder of knowing they aren't forgotten.

Secretly, one may appear confident and seem as if they have it all together, but give her a chance to speak her mind, and you will see that what glitters isn't always gold. The best gifts for those around you will be understanding their perspectives, and rather than giving advice, being present and listening attentively. The word 'endurance' can be sensitive for some because women have gone through those seasons for years and perhaps, going through internal pain they haven't been able to process properly; – an unexpected breakup, a called-off wedding; only they know…

According to the Ogilvy blog in their article; "Wellness Influences Got Real" (highly recommended read) emphasises on the importance of being authentic in the community and having a clear wellness strategy that will not only support branded partnerships, but build genuine relationships with each other. Source:

The Becoming Woman

https://www.ogilvy.com/ideas/wellness-influencers-got-real-where-are-brands#

Yes, this is about business relationships and influential leaders, however, from a relationship perspective, it's easy to be swayed or negatively influenced by the demand of society's pressures of scrolling through social media feeds and subconsciously comparing ourselves to other people that *seem* to have it all together. We judge by a post uploaded on Instagram or a video on TikTok that looks professional, attractive and has many likes and attention, and yet, we are oblivious to the fact that they too have their own secret battles.

It's very easy for influencers to burn out - despite the accolades and titles, they are human and have needs. I salute the influential women who are making an impact in their communities because it takes a level of grace to look after yourself without losing who you are.

I reflect on Apostle Paul and how he encouraged himself in 1 Corinthians 15:10 where he said that he worked harder than any of the other apostles, yet it wasn't his own strength but God who was working through Him by Grace – *emphasis added*. How many of us can confidently say we are allowing the Lord to work through and in us during the single season? I believe that when you don't put unnecessary pressure on yourself to be where you 'think' you ought to be, you become lighter and able to focus on your life.

Remember that you are enough, even if you don't hear it from other people.

In those moments of discovery, we develop a mindset of self-awareness, reminding ourselves that we are more than where we are; this starts with how we position ourselves and is a personal decision that one should make to not only protect their mental wellbeing, but being productive in the seasons of waiting. It is important to remind ourselves that we have the power to break negative cycles that people or our environments define us in. I ask you today, what sort of practical ways are you growing and making yourself available to

The Becoming Woman

those who are going through similar circumstances? When many are praised and being celebrated for their engagements or wedding day, another person could have fewer likes or attraction for various reasons; for example, starting a new online business, raising money for charity via GoFundMe or Crowdfunding etc. However, for the person who is starting their online business, that is what keeps them focused and intentional about where their life is heading to rather than being pressured to pursue a relationship in the name of *'settling'* or *'making others happy.'*

The becoming woman isn't intimidated because she's not yet engaged or dating, but is focused on her purpose and what she's called to do in her season. Be reminded that seasons change and where you are today will be different in the years to come.

Look at your life; study it and go back to 10, 20 or 30 years. Some of us have experienced the same or similar level of pain, anguish, anxiety and even fear which robs us of our futures that we can't seem to understand why we are in the same position up till now. Romans 12:2 is a love letter to not be moved or persuaded by what the world wants us to do, but renew our minds in a way that produces healthier patterns in our relationships with others and be focused.

Many women are in seasons where it's challenging to see a way clear, not because they choose to stay that way, but where their focus is at, and for this reason, it can bring a *feeling* of embarrassment, resentment and unwanted envy.

To be single at the age you deem to be married can trigger your heart. The question is: 'Who created this mental block?' Are you feeding your mind with the right thoughts and speaking life into your situation? If we aren't careful, we will become easily led by what we feel and questioning what is happening in our lives.

To question your season of singleness is to forfeit the lesson that it desires to teach you.

As those who are pressured from time to time, it is natural to question why the demand on marriage is becoming such a norm with excess finances being spent and going beyond our financial means

The Becoming Woman

for the wedding itself. Remember that the wedding is one day, but marriage is for a lifetime. We can't always blame the pressure of social media because people choose what they want to post. Nonetheless, we have to be responsible for how we come across towards what we see online and how we process our thoughts that cause us to be the way we do.

We ought to be encouraged that singleness is a rich blessing that can't be compromised by anything else. Becoming woman; you deserve better, so hold on and be expectant. It is also reassuring for God who says in Genesis that it is not good for man to be alone has already got someone in mind for you, so let this be your joy. God will continue to wait for you until your values and self-perception aligns with His. We should start using our time to become better versions of ourselves.

There is a difference between being publicly visible and working on yourself privately. Before the public show is revealed, there has to be private work going on behind the scenes. Yes, it will be long, frustrating and tiring, but anything that is going to bring great value will be tested and tried before coming out as gold. You can only be in denial for a certain period of time before you choose to accept that you need *real change*.

Depending on your upbringing and the environment you're in can also play a contributing factor in how you see yourself. No matter who you are, there will always be someone to indirectly ask "So…how's *life?*" – those eyes that roll at the back of your head knowing what the person means. It isn't a surprise at all because as far as I am concerned, we can all be nosey from time to time.

Maybe you are a single mother who finds it hard bringing up your only child or children; it could be a loved one leaving you feeling used or purposeless. People change; the world is changing, relationships are changing, and the only way it's going to get better is when we renew our minds and accept the season of endurance.

Renewing your mind is an inner work you have to take responsibility on. No one can renew your mind the way you can. It is far better to influence people than for people to influence you, because this comes with a cost. Whoever has your ear has the opportunity to either push you to greatness or remind you of the past.

The impulses, inclinations and instincts of the mind are at your core. We must inform our minds that we are bigger than what we

The Becoming Woman

think about and use wisdom to handle it. Do not allow people to define who you are, because it's not what people say that defines you, but what you speak into your life that defines you. The becoming woman erases the distractions that try to hold her back.

When there is temptation to talk about someone's failed relationship, the best gift you can give is to say a prayer or kind word about the situation because you never know what can happen in life. Hearing news like this must always keep us humble and not look down on those who are going through those vulnerable and difficult seasons. Heartbreak isn't for the faint hearted and it will take time to heal, and for this reason, women need to continue genuinely serving, supporting, cherishing, caring and honouring one another as much as possible.

There is great power in sisterhood and shouldn't be taken lightly. It may not necessarily come in large batches of 10, but could be two ordained sisters that can hold you up when you feel like your world is falling apart.

Psalm 147:3 reminds us that God will continually heal the hearts of those who are broken and will bind up their wounds. As a woman who is becoming, only you know the pain you've been through. It can be tempting to blame the other person, but what character traits have we identified in ourselves? Have we truly healed from the previous relationships and used that pain to draw us closer to God?

Another focus point that comes to mind is 'What is your purpose for being in a relationship?' When it comes to purposeful relationships, how does your relationship enlighten the community? What is it about your relationship that makes it different from all the others? It is essential that we support each other on the journey of life, particularly when we desire to be in a relationship without losing who we are in the process.

The endurance of singleness prepares you for the next level which isn't to be taken lightly. Singleness is a gift that when used appropriately, will eventually benefit others within the environment. Whether you are frustrated about the wait and how others are excelling in their relationships, take the time to work and build strong connections with your friendships. In essence, it can be easy to assume that once we've reached a certain level in our career path, our business or financial status that we are ready to jump into a relationship. There are tendencies we can often face in terms of questioning our current position and where we ought to be by now.

No matter the level or status of your life, it doesn't signify or represent your end. When it comes to knowing your purpose, it will require taking the time to understand and know yourself. In 2014, I started an online women's blog as a supportive forum to encourage young women dealing with various issues, and at the time, I didn't realise my purpose was slowly unfolding. I shared experiences with other women who were going through similar challenges and wanted to see freedom and healing take place, not realising the blog enabled me to publish my first book *It's Time to Heal – A Woman's Journey to Self-Discovery and Freedom*.

Through this book, it's given access to speak with other women at events and being able to run my own workshops and seminars. It wasn't just an amazing feeling; it was the season of being fully obedient and submissive. Did I still have thoughts of being with someone? Yes, I did, however, that didn't deter me from what I was called to do. Most times, we are eager to focus on 'what's next' rather than enjoying the present moment. Had I not taken advantage of the present season in front of me, I don't believe my first book would've been written, neither would it have fit the purpose for this new book.

It's in the becoming stages that you find out who you are and what's on the inside of you. There is no time for wandering or second-guessing yourself. A confident woman is sure of who she is and able to endure seasons of waiting. We must be aware that if we don't guard our hearts, we open the door to comparison of what our relationships should 'look like' because of what we see, and therefore neglect the importance of working on ourselves and building confidence within.

What one relationship can handle may not always be what another relationship can handle.

In the times we are living in, the greatest gift to the community is serving. I will not forget what a friend told me as she mentioned

The Becoming Woman

these words: "If you want to be married, serve a married couple." I truly understood every word that was shared, and coming from a place of waiting, it made sense to apply this wisdom into my own life. The beauty is that you are receiving direct wisdom from couples who are ahead of you and can teach what you need to know and prepare for the future.

From a Biblical point of view, Jesus put many people first before Himself and carried the burdens of those who were vulnerable. When you are in the season of waiting, there will always be many opportunities to serve the community. From a place of genuine concern, you will gain strength to remind your sisters that waiting is only for a period, and that their desires will change, nonetheless, there will also be moments where rest needs to be applied.

In the book of John 6:15, Jesus discerned the crowd as they wanted to take Him by force and make Him king, however, He withdrew *again* to the mountain by Himself." The word 'again' tells us that Jesus made a regular daily practice of withdrawing from the crowd in order to pray. To be effective in the season of singleness, we must learn to be comfortable with ourselves.

A confident woman is in the process of becoming. She isn't waiting for people to approve of her; rather she finds her strength and worth in focusing on what she can do as a single woman. We must take the example of the becoming woman who stands on her own two feet, and not influenced by the movements of others. She isn't competing or worried, but knows the beauty that peace brings when she enjoys her own company. The secret to success lies in knowing what God has assigned and gifted you to do in the season of singleness.

It may seem difficult to stand, especially when you don't feel like you've accomplished enough. The world has their own perceptions of success by telling you to follow their customs. Our greatest lesson for the future is to keep moving. Stagnation has nothing to do with endurance. With endurance, you can move mountains, shake nations, become better, work on yourself and, more importantly, be present.

The pressure women go through could also be caused by their own self-limiting beliefs or the constant focus on what others are doing or achieving. You are what you dwell on, and it's not enough to assume that our environments cause us to act a certain way. There

The Becoming Woman

has to be a level of mature accountability in the way you consume information. If this is the case, how can we make sound decisions when emotions are speaking on our behalf? We are capable of putting healthy boundaries in place.

This is the perfect opportunity to get closer to God and hear what He has to say. The real challenge is when you are influenced by positivity and critics at the same time. It's easy for someone to ask "When will your time come?" and you respond by saying; "When God steps in!" It has nothing to do with anyone's opinion for what is yours. Great blessings that come from God are in His appointed time (Ecclesiastes 3:11). The time it takes to invest in your growth is for a lifetime, so make the most of the single season and fall greatly in love with Your Father who knows everything about you.

People's opinions of you doesn't define you, unless <u>you</u> allow them to.

It is expensive to base your identity on societal standards. In essence, when it becomes a challenge to embrace contentment in the single season, it can be easy to fill the void with overworking, distracting yourself by watching movies, going out and spending money on unnecessary items, not having boundaries or even the most popular, being a people-pleaser. Despite the distractions, you must ask yourself why you desire to be in a relationship whilst appreciating and embracing the season of singleness. I want you to answer the following questions and read them back to yourself. With all you've been reading thus far:

1) Are you mentally, emotionally, spiritually and physically ready to be in a relationship? If yes, why? If no, why?

_____

_____

_____

_____

The Becoming Woman

2) Do you still speak with your past exes? If yes, why?

3) Are you ready to open your heart to the opposite sex about your past?

4) Do you know the importance of loving yourself before allowing another man to love you?

The Becoming Woman

_____

_____

_____

_____

_____

5) Are you truly happy and content in your single season?

_____

_____

_____

_____

_____

6) Out of 10, (1 being unsatisfactory, 5 being neutral and 10 being very satisfactory) how is your relationship with money?

_____

_____

_____

_____

_____

The Becoming Woman

These questions are extremely important during the season of endurance and being open about where you are. You are making a healthy decision to decide whether you are ready for the next stage. No one can tell you when you are ready; it is your responsibility to know. For this reason, you ought to have inner peace in your single season before seeking to be in a relationship.

Take the time to listen to yourself; whether it's about your past relationships, where you currently are in life or aren't sure how the future will look. The moment doubt or fear starts, it influences your decisions based on emotional fluctuations. Your emotions can't be your decision-maker. Don't allow your mind to worry about others looking at you differently because you are single. There is beauty in waiting for God's best, even when it feels slow. Greatness isn't to be rushed, so don't jump the season you are in. Instead, embrace the freedom to work within and take each day as it comes.

It's also important to remember the promises spoken over your life as it will help you relax in the present moment. Pray over those prophecies, especially the promises that focus on marriage and preparation. Make sure you nurture and protect what you hear to avoid contradicting voices.

Encouragement: in your single season of endurance, learn to invest and listen to sermons that align you to purpose and the ability to keep your mind at ease. Forcing anything to happen that isn't at the appointed time will be the outcome of your own strength. Anything that's in His Will shall last and will be evident to all that it was by Grace, not works, so that no one will boast *(Ephesians 2:8-9)*. Enduring singleness is a question you'd need to ask yourself from a place of honesty and what you're learning in the process.

Being single doesn't label you different to others, but is an opportunity to embrace what the season is teaching and preparing you for. In the single season, you aren't negotiating, you are evolving and becoming the woman you're called to be. Waiting well always produces the best results and a patient attitude will speak on your behalf.

Reflection: It's not how long you wait, but how <u>well</u> you wait patiently! *#TheBecomingWoman*.

The Becoming Woman

Chapter T.H.R.E.E.
-
Take a Break

"Explore new skills and embrace change."

Nature; ahhh; what a beauty! The awakening of a new dawn and the sunset gently rising to the setting down of the sun; the moon and stars glazing brightly in the sky at night. I absolutely love nature! When last did you take a walk from your busy schedule to be still, rest and just *be present*? A great gift to mankind is a well-deserved break. Your body needs it as well as your mind. We can all define breaks in various ways including having short power-naps, taking time off social media, journaling, travelling abroad, having long walks in the park, meditating and being still, practising mindfulness etc.

As a woman who is constantly positioning herself to be in a committed and fruitful relationship, there are many lessons to learn about essential breaks before committing to the opposite sex. A break enables you to work immensely on your own personal struggles, to remove yourself from the noises and distractions to discern whether they are coming from a healthy or unhealthy place. At some point in our lives, we'll have to step back and categorise those who help us on our journey to becoming better, relative to those who come and subtract from us.

In the book of John, due to the works Jesus accomplished, the people He was surrounded with placed a lot of pressure on Him because the anointing He had was beyond the crowd's imagination. I love a statement that Bishop TD Jakes said in a recent sermon: "The anointing you respect is the anointing you receive." There will be different types of people that are in your life to be nosey and find out what's going on, however, those who are genuinely there for you will come with pure motives without expecting anything else in return. They will also respect your boundaries and the gifts you possess.

The Becoming Woman

> **In life, if we don't learn how to take breaks from time to time, our bodies will make us learn how to.**

As much as I love cooking, I really enjoy using food as demonstrations for certain topics. Take an onion for example; when you cut the onion, it has many layers. It's vital to make sure that you get to the core of the issues in your life. These include distancing yourself from people who make you remember what you don't yet have. God can also reveal these to you in dreams and visions. Being able to identify the problems at the early stages is a strong sign that you are coming out of your situation and is the starting point of a healthy and balanced lifestyle.

From a social media perspective, your followers will only know what you share or post with them. Nonetheless, those who *you* follow won't always show their dark or vulnerable moments and this should help you to understand that it's not everything that life teaches you to expose to others unless God leads you to share.

When sharing good news, it is effective once the deed is completed and has come to pass. We must get to a stage where wisdom is used when making decisions, particularly with social media. As we know, technology is advancing every day and we are seeing an increase in the re-sharing of videos, screenshots, recording on other devices and saving them onto computers or laptops for later use. The Internet is large; you have every right to control your life on it!

There must also be wisdom when being vulnerable about your hardships. Even if it is coming from a place of encouragement, understanding the purpose behind sharing and taking it to God in prayer to ask if it's His Will for you to share with your followers is the first stage of maturity. Whether you have 100,000 followers or 1,000 followers on social media, the important lesson is to ensure what you desire to share is spoken of at the *right time*.

> **As a becoming woman, she will know what needs to be shared.**

The Becoming Woman

We are all different and unique in our respective ways, and the deeper circumstances we face can either be resolved by seeking God and being used by Him to share with us at the appointed time. No matter what happens throughout your life, learn how to take breaks from what you are attached to. Challenge yourself and take a year off your most used social platforms and see how much peace you will have. Surrendering what is taking your time leads to a healthy mindset and focused perspective. You don't need to entertain what isn't adding value to your life just to make time go quicker.

Social media is a platform with multiple purposes and intentions behind what it carries; it's not who you are, where you base your worth or something you turn to when finding solace, confirmation or approval. Be the individual that uses social media as a positive platform to encourage and inspire, therefore finding peace in your current season of taking breaks.

Whether you're a single woman seeking a life partner, it is important that you spend quality time with yourself. A great book I'd highly recommend when taking time away to reset is Dr. Gary Chapman's book 'The 5 Love Languages: The Secret to Love That Lasts.' This book helps to identify what your primary love language is out of the following:

1) Words of Affirmation
2) Quality Time
3) Acts of Service
4) Gifts
5) Physical Touch

Each of these love languages will give you an opportunity to identify where you fit and how to use it when working on yourself and your potential spouse. Self-love is important and all the 5 love languages gives an indication of how you can improve your own life before stepping into a relationship.

Social media shouldn't be used as a way to monitor ones' progress to compare.

The Becoming Woman

It's also important to be mindful that when you choose to take breaks, it helps you to rest from the usual community of friends because we all need to get to the place where we can be still and allow our minds to process thoughts without the interruption of others. For this reason, it is important to make a healthy habit of understanding the type of seasonal friends and acquaintances who are in your life, their purpose and role is.

Never confuse friendship categories and expect everyone to understand where you are going. No one has the power to change your mind, but you have the ability to ensure that who you are surrounded with are people who bring out the best in you and help you birth destiny.

There will be moments where God will place certain people in your life to confirm a word of encouragement and prepare you. Those moments are precious and God speaks in a gentle manner, so be sensitive when He wants to commune with you during your breaks. As you continue seeking God in faith, He will bring the relevant people into your life to confirm what you've communicated in prayers about. This is divine alignment of friendships, which I also define as 'spiritual covering or confirmation.'

You must learn to take healthy breaks from those who diminish your faith or question why you are stepping out in the season of singleness. You don't want to open the door to distractions and those who want you to wait until every area of your life indicates that you can move forwards.

> **Taking breaks is an essential sign of self-care, ease of mind, rest and reflection.**

You may be surrounded by environments which don't agree with your level of thinking, and going 'too ahead of yourself' when trying on wedding dresses as a 'single woman' however, that is where you must discern and gradually detach yourself from those voices. If they can't support you in your single season, don't expect support when you transition into marriage. Be mindful of the company you keep and don't allow yourself to be moved by what others are

The Becoming Woman

saying. The best way to silence the negative voices is to seek God privately, creating space for Him to minister to your heart. When the timing is right, you won't need to announce yourself because ordained destiny helpers will celebrate the goodness of God for you. Just continue being faithful; it may hurt for a while, but a time is coming for you to be noticed. God doesn't forget the tears of His daughters, especially when the pressure is intense.

As becoming women; we have to be selectively intentional about discerning and removing ourselves from environments which don't increase our value and ultimately end up living a double-minded life. I remember a friend so close to me who I cherished as a sister, but the closer we got, the friendship got intimately painful.

There were times where I was afraid to leave the house without greeting her, because fear gripped me of being my authentic self. It was as if I lost my identity because of a friend. I would always make an attempt to see how she was doing, but to no avail. She would give me the cold shoulder. What do you do when you try to reach out to someone you love, but they turn their back on you?

I am not the only one who has been through this experience; it's not easy, but if it hadn't been for the Lord who was on my side, I would not be the woman I am today. I am strong, I am tenacious, I am confident, but moreover, I am FREE to take healthy breaks from environments which don't serve my highest good and own it!

Building a mindset of freedom is a gradual process, and it starts with speaking out. When you communicate your feelings and vent out the frustrations, it releases the negative strongholds that keep you bound. For this reason, the more breaks that are implemented, the better it will be to position your mind to rest.

Let's get your mind thinking further; out of the two options, what is more important to you? Tick one box:

1) *Trying to please someone who God may be taking out of your life?* – a closed door is still an answered prayer ☐

2) *Pleasing God and allowing Him to bring the right people in your life?* – open your mind and heart to allow new people in; God knows how and who to use to bless you ☐

The Becoming Woman

When situations don't seem to match up and you sense your spirit dampening or being out of alignment, take the time to embrace nature and do what you can to soothe those distracting thoughts. Keeping your mind sane is a source of contributing to healthy breaks as well as journaling. We are becoming more open to certain situations at once that cause different forms of stagnation and fear.

Instead, we are able to tackle them head-on and see it as a way to persevere. If you are to reflect back on your life, the relationships you were in and what you entertained, you will understand how important breaks are to finding out what you truly desire in the opposite sex and being at a mature space to handle the next stage of a relationship.

Consistent breaks help in identifying what you will tolerate and how to be a positive influence to a society that is fond of avoiding the gradual stages of progress. I encourage you to be patient with yourself and enjoy the season you are in.

Perhaps you've attended many single events and thought it was your chance to be 'seen' by the other half. Nonetheless, you must come to the realisation that not every opportunity or event is for you. No matter how glamourous it looks online or how they promote it to get your attention, if it's not appealing to you, don't waste your precious time and feel the need to go for fear of missing out.

On the contrary, if you've encountered a relationship that has caused you to change countless of times, have a deep think about why you still intend to stay. Could it be that you are in the process of discovering yourself, and becoming more of who you've been called to be? Could it be stepping out of that toxic relationship to help you realise the person God destined for you to have?

The fear of being labelled as *lonely* is what one wants to avoid, but not realising that in the long run, it becomes difficult to break because the hold was too strong to let go of in the first place. Don't give any power or room to another individual to have authority over your life, who you should be with or where you should go.

It is possible to take a break from the dating scene and work on yourself. It's not every day swipe to the left! We should be mindful to remember that being alone doesn't equate to loneliness. Great expectations and results are birthed when you have quiet time to focus on what's going on internally. Listen to your body; listen to your mind. We should be at a stage where social media shouldn't dictate how far we ought to go or what we should be doing with our lives.

More importantly, having breaks with the One who wakes you up each morning is the first and foremost priority. We tend to forget that God is always around and fall into the deception that our alarm clocks wake us up, but it's His unconditional loving presence which gently taps us as we open our eyes to see another day.

Trying to be part of the world's standards isn't something to keep your focus on. When you try to be like others, you miss the opportunity to be blessed because your mind is clouded by what they do, and the pressure to imitate them. Let's be real; we all need breaks from a lot of distractions that take up time and instead, reflect on our lives, where we are at present and what we need to prepare for the future. One step at a time, ladies.

Freedom looks good on you and the beauty of life. Building relationships is taking the time to rest, reflect and just be. The seasons of having breaks can depend on what you aim to achieve. Some people may come off socials for a month and others for a year. Either way, we will require community to be around us when transitioning into the next level. For you to embrace the beauty of breaks and be happy with where you are, it is essential to remind yourself that every situation is only for a short period of time, however, it can become longer when constantly worrying and looking back on what you surrendered.

Surrendering social media to get your focus back is a great positive influence for your mental and emotional wellbeing. Taking the time to stop binging on other people's stories or watching so much content on wedding dresses, décor, venues, MUA's, etc; all these beautiful blessings will come at the appointed time.

> **Taking yourself out of God's Will to find your own way in seeking a relationship will cause confusion and delay.**

Anything that hasn't been consulted with God in addition to misusing your time is slowly detrimental. Your mind is precious and

The Becoming Woman

how you look after it determines the conversations you have and what you hear.

Soul ties can be formed when our thoughts are focused on the past; perhaps you were in a relationship with a man that promised to marry you, however, it didn't happen, so you keep watching his every move, stories, who he's seeing, and eventually, you're slowly decreasing in spirit and strength. This is a very strong soul tie for vulnerable women who are yet to discover themselves. When your feelings make you focus on the man you thought loved you, take breaks and ask God to expose your divine destiny helpers who will cause you to remain focused.

To the becoming woman who uses multiple dating apps and attends various networking events, learn to take breaks from them all. Taking breaks doesn't mean you're lacking in faith; it helps you to think logically about the purpose behind your decisions. Remember that every decision made must come from a healthy mindset.

In the upcoming chapters, we will focus on the beauty of seasons and the key lessons learnt along the way, because what you embrace is what you are able to change and transition into new levels of growth. These new levels of growth require patience, a focused and disciplined mindset and remembering who you are.

As you are growing, there will be open doors, opportunities to travel, settling down in a committed relationship, career changes, seeking new business ventures etc, which all require gradual steps. Rushing the process doesn't allow you to be your best self, rather, it makes it difficult to track your performance, remembering that great results are formed in the beauty of taking breaks. It would be detrimental to your wellbeing in working long hours without having a break. Those moments of quietness and ease allow you to listen to the environments you're in and make clear decisions to benefit your growth.

When you are in a season of 'waiting' to be found or being noticed by the wrong attention, that is what will gravitate itself to you. The becoming woman who has confidence in herself is finding ways to improve her life privately before she becomes a public influencer. She wants to add value in the lives of others without compromising her worth or settling for second best. Now over to you: what is it that you can do to take time out and constantly work on the areas

The Becoming Woman

you've been hiding? Remember that a man who wants to be with you already sees you as a confident woman. Overtime and with wisdom, having transparent conversations will be very essential. Being fully healed from the past and developing self-control over your environments are pivotal moments of success that should be celebrated.

Getting your mind around holiday seasons, going to the cinema alone, treating yourself to essential skincare products, booking dinner for one etc, are all forms of self-care. When the becoming woman doesn't take breaks, she rushes the beauty of what the season is teaching her, and is easily restless to wait for the man God has ordained to find her. Despite the busyness of life, refuse to come to a place where you choose to remain stagnant, neither allow social media or your own limiting thoughts to get the best of you. As the years are going by, we must learn the importance of choosing what to hold onto and what to let go of.

It is good to relax your mind from the distractions that have persuaded you to look at what others are doing and comparing your journey to those around you. Remember that the person you may be looking at or comparing yourself to have their own battles to fight. What breaks can teach you, distractions can't. There are seasons where working smart is essential, but there are also seasons where rest is good to rejuvenate the body and mind. Naps are also part of your wellbeing and breaks; when last did you have a power nap?

The becoming woman must learn to identify the difference between internal and external distractions and must be dealt with in gentle correction, and identifying the unreliable emotions that make us react harshly to others for no apparent reason. We all go through various seasons of growth, and although it does come with painful moments, we must learn how to take essential breaks from situations and environments that make us shrink or hide who we are for fear of being misunderstood.

The becoming woman is confident not only in her own company, but in the Presence of God. That is her biggest strength!

The Becoming Woman

The temptation to become angry with a friend or someone you thought loved you will influence your character over anything else. Learn how to slow down and *think* before you react. Filter through your thoughts and ask yourself whether you are being irrational. Is it worth losing your mind over a situation that doesn't make you better?

During the different stages of life, you will learn that having one or two trusted friends is a rich blessing to continue the journey of becoming. A friend who sees you at your greatest and lowest moments is an answered prayer. The key more than anything else is allowing the Holy Spirit to help you open up at the right time. He will keep you from ruining meaningful friendships and relationships that are placed in your life for your personal development.

From the timeframe of my dating journey, I haven't seen it fitting or applicable to date several men at once to determine who was 'the one.' Women will have their preferences when it comes to dating and how many men they'd like to *interview* at once, however, coming from the perspective of committing to one man that's ready and available to take the relationship to the next level will require a healthy balance of rest.

Let's continue: May 2019, the last time I promised myself I'd attend another single's networking event! Moving forwards a few years later and as an engaged woman, I take into account the beauty of learning from those vulnerable moments where it seemed that nothing was happening, and although I was constantly stepping out and being social, I couldn't understand why nothing was happening.

At the time, I was writing books and encouraging the community in sharing their stories despite the number of posts appearing on social media for being in a relationship. Having seen those posts, it made me want to know God even more. I had the choice to either allow what I heard to shake my faith, or use it to strengthen the relationship with my first love.

Take a look back over your life and be real with yourself. How many single events did you attend because you wanted to know who 'the one' was? There's a constant groan in the soul when we attend events but find out that God's purpose didn't reside at that event. Remember how you choose to process your thoughts is a strong weapon that should protect your heart because not every invitation needs to be acknowledged.

The Becoming Woman

For those who know what I am talking about, you already know! There's a level of faith that leaps up and embraces the beauty of waiting for the best, nonetheless, there will be triggering moments where you can become tired of the repetition in meeting the same or similar faces and not developing genuine relationships with at least one person from that networking event.

Ladies, your time is precious and highly valued. Add tax on your time and be intentional about where you are going. I am mindful of what events and networking opportunities I attend because although it may look good, it may not necessarily be good for me.

From a place of healthy wellbeing and a mindset that's able to pivot, these short and long-term breaks are vital, so embrace them to the fullest. It may not have to be extravagant, but you still need rest. The moments where you're able to create beautiful memories with your girlfriends when travelling abroad and soaking up each moment of every day can't be utilised effectively when your mind is constantly wanting to be with someone else.

Those breaks with your sisters are there to strengthen, encourage and enable you to grow into a better woman. You are still on a journey and those breaks are for you to maximise and grab every nutrient you need to build a healthy outcome. That outcome is a reflection of your character and integrity. Don't rush or give up too soon, because greatness opens its doors in unexpected ways.

In summary, it's humbling to remember that we won't always know our next steps, and that is the beauty of having faith in a God who knows what tomorrow holds. You can take breaks and enjoy His Presence as He fills you with peace and all-round reassurance, reminding you that identity isn't found in the busyness of life, but in the quiet and solitude environments where you can be led by the still waters and lie down in green pastures. Take the time to rest because your future self will thank you for it.

Reflection: Sis; enjoy the breaks and don't for a second look back at what you think you're missing. Your best days are ahead of you! #*TheBecomingWoman*.

The Becoming Woman

Chapter F.O.U.R. -

Unbroken

"A woman who is unbroken by her past is an overcomer – she may have cracks, but she's able to build herself up again. She is the resilient unbroken woman."

Unbroken is the woman who has been tested by many trials but not crushed. She's the woman who has made an intentional decision to be free from the pain and mistakes of the past. In some areas in our lives, we are somewhat broken, and this is a positive sign that we need God, not just for Him to solve our problems, but to use them to draw us closer.

There's so much emphasis on relationships, particularly in society that most people tend to misuse as a way to fill a deep void or refuse to confront those stubborn areas in our lives. It could be from their past and the way they've been treated by someone they once loved…

Being unbroken is God's way of saying 'I am here and will strengthen you *if* you allow me to'. No matter how talented we are, we aren't built to do everything on our own. Whether it's setting up a new business venture, being called into full-time ministry, being a wife and mother, which are all successful blessings, we still need His guidance and leading.

Story time: I saw a lady walking across the street crying. She got on the train at 14:32pm towards Victoria. I saw her walk to the nearest seat as she sat alone and started to sob the more. I decided to sit two seats away in case she didn't want any confrontation. A few moments later, I gently approached her, and rather than me speaking, I comforted her by putting my arm around her back asking the Holy Spirit to guide and lead me on what to say.

It was that moment where silence was the best answer for the type of situation she was in. She didn't stay on the train for long, and I was thinking of what to say in case she arrived at her destination quicker than expected. As she got off, she looked at me, wiped her tears, smiled and said; 'thank you.' I knew it was only the power of God who enabled her to come off smiling.

> **Our tears paint a picture to the One who knows us; our tears will never be wasted.**

One of the greatest lessons I've learnt about those who are unbroken is that tears are their power. The becoming woman may not need to talk about what she's going through; only at the appointed time. The beautiful lesson about being unbroken is that no matter what you are going through, you have the power to use every season of brokenness to make you complete. When you are confronted with a situation that you never expected to happen, what is your first response? Oftentimes, the words 'be still' comes to mind for the woman who knows the importance of intimately drawing closer to God, and seeking Him for strength, clarity and confirmation.

We may assume we are okay, until we receive news that nearly makes our faith shatter. Anytime you've been hurt, it determines the state of your character and how you handle situations. Not everyone is able to handle certain seasons of pain, and this could be for various reasons. The becoming woman is intentional about being in a state of ease and normalcy because she knows how it feels to be out of balance. She takes a deep breath in and then exhales out **#phew!**

As women with many talents, gifts and skills, we have to benefit and contribute to our community and identify the key areas in our lives relating to building genuine relationships with friends and the potential spouse in order to create healthy connections.

When I look back over my life and remember the people God enabled me to cross paths with, it gave me a sense of purpose to serve them. At the time, I wasn't fully aware of my purpose, but I knew God had a plan for me to serve and encourage women to heal from within. We know that healing takes time and is a sensitive topic when it comes to opening up. For this reason, it's important as the becoming woman to know when to speak and when to be silent.

Listening in particular is an important yet *overlooked* skill as we become eager to put our perspectives across.

The Becoming Woman

We rather want to speak than understand and listen to the other person's point of view. Being unbroken is the ability to listen to another woman's pain, whilst depending on God to help in dealing with your own. Some women are capable of handling their circumstances very well; not to say they don't have days of sorrow or heartache; they intentionally decide not to allow the weight of what they are going through to influence their lifestyle.

> **No matter how many women you are looking at, just know they have scars you'd never know of...**

It's one potential blockage to entertain thoughts that make you complacent, lazy, or even worse; settle and accept where you are as the mind struggles with various thoughts which produce negative outcomes. Becoming older and wiser continually teaches me to embrace every thought and take control of the negative blockages that devalue my mental and emotional wellbeing. Why would I give my mind the pain of distraction when it costs so much to build a positive mindset?

Do you remember when you'd say or entertain the following thoughts:

- *Will I ever get married?*

- *I'm getting old and the pressure is heaping up on me!*

- *Why can't I find a man that will understand 'my' needs?*

- *I can't be bothered with men anymore! They are not worth my time...*

Where are these words coming from? Are they from previous experiences? As a becoming woman, you have to be intentionally wise about the thoughts you invite especially in seasons of brokenness. Out of the abundance of the heart, the mouth speaks and

The Becoming Woman

what you say is what you will have. Even in anger, you can choose to be silent and practise being still. Meditate on what adds value in your life. I can only speak for those who understand not only the beauty of brokenness, but has learnt how to cherish, embrace and open up to it more.

I was in seasons where nothing appeared to make clear pathways; from having revelations of learning how to protect my thoughts, and being prayerful when others were in their own seasons of celebration causing me to desperately yearn for the Lord further. I didn't have any choice but to cry out to Jesus as I remember kneeling down in my late sister's room singing 'Miracle Worker' by JJ Hairston and Youthful Praise.

August 2020 was my breakthrough season. In that same year, revelations and visions started becoming very consistent. God used specific people to confirm what I was seeking the Lord for in my quiet time. It felt so unreal, but I decided to lean into it to the extent where I started laughing like Sarah in the Bible when God promised her a child at an old age in Genesis 18:12-15.

In due season, God will show you that the promises of abundant blessings are coming and you have to be ready for them. That's when you know you're near your breakthrough!

> **Don't let impatience or the perception of God make you lose what He promised you.**

When you can't pass the test of perseverance, your faith ceases to activate into what it's meant to do. In the broken seasons, you have the choice to increase your faith, despite not seeing the final results or outcomes. As the becoming woman emerges into the best version of herself, it is vital to remember that nothing great is birthed alone. The test of perseverance and being unbroken are two vital components in a woman's life journey to growth.

We must be sensitive to the fact that there is only so much which can be accomplished in a certain amount of time. No matter how strong we believe we are, breakdown season is coming, and when it arrives, don't ignore or suppress it trying to be 'Miss Independent.'

The Becoming Woman

Pride is a source of long-term heartache when we can't find the words or means to express how we truly feel, which is why as a becoming woman, it is exceedingly crucial to choose and select people who add value and refrain from those who are liabilities.

When you ask for help, it gives you a lightness in your soul; *"Hey sis, I hope you are well today? At this moment in time, I'm feeling low in spirit and mind; can you please help by praying for me in your spare time?"* A friend that can intercede for you in your lowest moments are those who are qualified to celebrate you in your highest achievements. It is important to uplift our sisters, particularly those who are aware of their own weaknesses in order to grow from them.

We need to be surrounded by positive people, because hard times are ready to test your character and integrity, but with the right support system, you are on the journey to being the unbroken woman.

It was 17:35pm on Tuesday 21st April 2015; a work colleague of mine was having a discussion about university life and its relevance. I'm not sure how the topic came up, but as we were speaking, she informed me that she'd lost her father a few months ago. Although we have parted ways in good faith, it hit me so much that when I saw this beautiful woman, I wouldn't have thought it because she was such a pleasure and joy to be around.

Her smile, sense of humour and work ethic revealed the beauty of a strong woman; a woman who knows her strength isn't in what she does, but in the confidence of God. We may not have a front row seat or the full privilege of knowing about ones' life or the inner pain of what one goes through until they choose to let it out.

This lady refused to be comforted by her teachers and friends. As I continued listening, the vibe I got from her was 'life goes on.' Indeed, life does go on, however, a gentle word came to me which was to stay close to her mother and younger brother; to love them, work hard for them, and continue the legacy of her late father.

An unbroken woman going through loss doesn't have the time to entertain unfruitful relationships.

The Becoming Woman

A confident woman is mindful not to entertain the spirit of jealousy and is the reason why we must attack this negative trait at the early stages, for we can't expect to receive in our own lives what we are unwilling to celebrate in the lives of others, especially when they have waited patiently. To the becoming woman, what has made you break down that tried to rob you of destiny and purpose?

One of the greatest moments in anyone's life is when they are able to release their emotions in a healthy way. This is where wisdom comes in; when we open up to one another, we release the weight that so easily entangles us from reaching our true God-given destiny.

God said in His Word that He came for us to enjoy and have life abundantly in reference to John 10:10. Our lives are testimonies for others who watch us. When you experience heartbreak, rejection or betrayal; people are watching the way you talk, how mature you are, the moves you make and how you conduct yourselves when the pain becomes unbearable. From a relationship perspective, they are watching how you pick yourself up from the rejection that once had power over you.

A wise word of encouragement: if you're recovering from a bad relationship, it's a mistake to rush into another one. No matter how you feel, the season will pass and eventually, you will be able to move on and embrace your life. The choice of being in a relationship is not about filling a void because you are alone or desperate to be in need, because when you don't value your single season and you continue making plans without rest, you will attract people who won't value you, nor your time because they have quick access to you. Learn to be discreet.

When it comes to boundaries, it is about valuing your space and time; don't allow anyone to come in and out of your life in an unordered fashion.

Make a mental note of this: *It's vital to live a pleasant and selfless life*:

- ***Pleasant*** – life is to be enjoyed regardless of what private and public battles come to find you.

- ***Selfless life*** – to live a servitude lifestyle that doesn't cause you to forget your role on earth. Not to be served, but to serve.

The Becoming Woman

Life isn't surrounded by you alone but many people with broken scars; some you will know and some you will never know. These moments should encourage the times where we come together to be real; take off the make-up, the eyelashes, the wigs and get to business! If you need to cry, let it out! Those tears will thank you later, and yes, those ugly cries are what is needed to refresh the soul. Hibernating and taking responsibility to manage and discipline your mind before the pain tries to take the lead is crucial to the woman on the healing journey.

As an unbroken woman who is becoming, she is always thinking about her life, where she is heading towards in the near future and what strategies she'll implement to keep herself going. Our words must be life, not just to ourselves, but to others who are surrounded by us because the becoming woman carries great value. Once she is out of alignment, she opens the door to be influenced by what she sees, hears or reads.

Empowering other women should be your top priority when you encounter seasons of brokenness. It's easy to hibernate and become independent, thinking you don't need or trust anyone. When those seasons come, take the time to write out in a journal all that's in your mind and what is trying to feed your emotions. Remember that in seasons of vulnerability, your emotions can't be trusted, which is why making healthy decisions when you have a clear head is better than hasty conclusions with a clouded mind.

It is good to think about yourself and work on personal growth, however, we are reminded as women who are called to impact nations and local communities to come back strong and help our sisters who really need it. There are some people who God will bring in your life because they are weak and need your expertise. Don't take this lightly because God will only reveal those He can trust you to manage. God grants the right people to add value in your life, so cherish and hold them tight.

> **Don't give everyone a front row seat if they haven't paid the price to watch the show.**

The Becoming Woman

You will encounter people who don't necessarily feel ready or want to open up for fear of being judged or laughed at. Once a post or video goes out, who knows whether it's been recorded from another device, stored on their phones and saved for the day you fall and become disgraced in public. Regardless of what they do with what you own, remember, God writes your story, not them!

Sometimes when you are going through your worst season, it's easy to remember those you put down, but when everything is working in your favour, pride starts settling in. No matter where you are in life; whether you are wealthy or financially insufficient, whether you have good dress sense or not, don't think of yourself as better than anyone else. You don't know when their opportunity of progress will come, and if you're not careful, you may close the door on a blessing that was meant to be for you from the person you underestimated.

Whether she is working in a retail store 40 hours a week or choosing to be a stay-at-home mum, don't give pride a foothold to rob you of your blessings because you refuse to humble yourself. This applies to relationships as well; we shouldn't take anyone for granted and assume that how we see them at face value is how they'll always be for the rest of their lives. We must learn to give people grace and the time to evolve and discover who they've been called to be. If you aren't adding value in their lives, please don't waste their time! Leave them alone so God will align them to the people they need to be surrounded by.

Opening up enlightens burdens when done in wisdom and at the appointed time. I am not saying that you should be unwise and spread yourself thin to allow anyone to access you without paying a price, but be led by the Spirit to open up to those God reveals and those you believe can be trusted. As you yearn and draw closer to the Lord, He starts showing you what is on His heart, and when you speak to Him about any situation, He will make it clear to you. No matter what you are going through or how you are feeling, God understands you transparently. He knows how painful it is to be broken.

Allowing God to heal you is a sign of growth and an opportunity of open doors to change and grow into the becoming woman. You are not only growing in wisdom, but you are also growing spiritually. The moment you are about to receive your greatest breakthrough, thoughts of guilt, the voice of enemies and low self-esteem tries to enter your mind causing you to stay stagnant. When those moments come, learn to open your mouth and release it to the Lord in prayer. Don't assume that it's best to be silent and not speak about it.

To add on this, I knew my faith was being tested in several areas, but the joy of His Presence, sermons and positive words over my life kept me going. When you are in an environment of brokenness, God starts to gradually reveal Himself in stages. At times, when it seemed difficult, all I could do was seek God intensely and wait for an answer. Without me realising, God used certain people to confirm what I needed to hear.

I refused to entertain confusion and have a 'comfortable answer' just to soothe my temporary emotions. I was willing to wait for a solid word that upheld me, and I tell you; it's the best experience you will encounter when you do it His way. There are times in your downfalls that faith will be tested. Faith is the assurance of what you desire without seeing it. Your faith is present to help you walk in victory and, at times, when we encounter certain problems, there is a tendency to fight back in our own strength, not realising that God's power is not your power.

The becoming woman is discovering who God created her to be, not doubting His power or ability to work. Do not feel the need to fight everything by yourself. Just rest. I know it can be hard and you will not always understand the way God works, but you must remember that God hears you.

I use this as a reference – in an exam hall before the test starts, the invigilators ask students if they need spare pens and paper; that is the only time they will communicate. Once the invigilator says "You can now begin the exam!", they are silent because you are in the testing season. This is how God works.

Even though He doesn't speak directly to our situations, we must be still and allow Him to lead. Patience is a virtue and can only be effective when we don't take matters in our own hands. We get tired from time to time because we are focused on the problem that we don't take the time to pray. The more we pray, the less we worry.

When God picks you in your broken state, life gradually begins to change. He carves you into who you are meant to be and will prepare you for who He has. He wants you to leave the former to

The Becoming Woman

accept the latter. Look back over your life and reflect on the former ways you entertained. The negative thoughts and environments which didn't bring out the best in you; they all become strange because you've been there for a length of time and becomes uncomfortable because you're yearning for better.

Your environment begins to look different; people won't understand you or your ways (which is a great benefit when you look at it from a freedom perspective), and eventually, you'll start to see that what was comfortable in one area doesn't align in another, especially if it isn't in His Will for you. When the broken shame is finally off, you'll agree that the process was worth it, and endurance was the best choice because its moulded you into the woman God created you to be.

The woman you are today is opening abundant doors for better blessings and once surrendered to the Father, it will become a living testimony! It will be a masterpiece for other women to see the power of God and what He is capable of doing.

In times of brokenness, it's easy to entertain thoughts of negativity, doubt and low self-esteem. The comparison starts to appear and becomes difficult to see yourself the way God does. "Am I really good enough?" Those words start to occur and if we are not careful, comparing yourself to someone will end up becoming an idol. Be the woman who uses her pain and turn it into purpose.

Everything you've been through will never be wasted and although we can handle certain situations better than others, the more broken you are, the wiser you become, especially as you are getting closer to your breakthrough.

Don't come out of alignment sis; stay where you are and fill your mind with the promises of God to keep on top of your brokenness.

Reflection: It's when I am broken, that's when I am strong. I didn't realise that brokenness builds wholeness within. I control what I hear and refuse to entertain what isn't for me. I know my worth and in due course, I will rise above every hurt and frustration. For now, I am healing and getting better each day because I know my best days are ahead of me!
#TheBecomingWoman.

Chapter F.I.V.E.

-

The Courting Process

"Transitioning takes time; it's about resilience, focus and embracing the beauty of evolving."

A private and intimate part of life is in the word *transition*. When you study this word, what comes to mind? Sometimes, we get comfortable and don't want to entertain any form of change, however, there is beauty in transitioning. A wise individual says that once you've stopped learning, you've stopped growing. It is important not to dismiss or rush what the changing seasons are preparing you for.

As we are inspired and influenced by what we see, it's easy to rush the present moment, not embracing that the present moment is the starting ground to creating a beautiful harvest. Think about a seed that's hidden in the ground. You don't see it because the soil protects the seed. It eventually needs nurturing and the owner provides water for the seed to grow. When all is said and done, there is a sense of peace that comes when we leave the seed to do what it needs to do.

I use this process to remind you that no matter how hidden you feel right now, there is a time for you to blossom. It may not come when you want it, but will arrive at the appointed time. From a relationship perspective, I am not an expert on *courting*, however, having been around a few people that have and are currently going through this stage has made it easy to share key lessons when being in the season of singleness and opening up to courting.

When you hear the word *courting*, what comes to mind? Suddenly, you come on social media and see a woman who has changed her status from 'single' to 'in a relationship.' What is your first response?

Overtime, we realise that life changes and therefore, we become more private in our movements. When you are secure in a relationship, it's easy to keep a low-profile, particularly those who

The Becoming Woman

want to start out at a slow pace. As we are becoming wiser, we must be aware that the courting stages will change. The courting stage is an opportunity to know who you are. It's the time to invest in all areas of your life, from financial development to emotional intelligence, physical health to spiritual and mental wellbeing and other contributing factors, especially building your own life and becoming whole in the process.

The beauty of courting can be seen from two perspectives:

1) It can be done privately between you and your partner and;

2) For the man who is pursuing a woman discreetly before making it public.

Notice I didn't say *women*. As the man, being the pursuer comes with purpose-led intentions. Being open in getting to know one woman on a friendly level is the starting point. When a man fixates his focus on the woman he believes is for him, he will continue becoming more intentional about her. Yes, the dating and courting game has changed over the years, but the principle of pursuing *the one* attracts many today, particularly Godly relationships that lead to peace of mind and a healthy balance of love, laughter and enjoyment (because who says Godly relationships are boring!?)

When the courting stage begins, we all have different perspectives on how it should be. Depending on your preferences, you will know what is best and how you'd like to be pursued. For example, some may like to be pursued in social settings where there's light snacks, good music and a calmness in the atmosphere.

Someone is able to break the ice and therefore becomes easier to adapt and interact with others. Regardless of what's been portrayed online, there are still Godly and mature, stable men who are intentional about settling down and being in a relationship.

Being around family members and enquiring about counselling and therapy sessions sets the foundation in the courting process. Start gently and build a genuine friendship to determine whether you are compatible – this stage is highly important and shouldn't be rushed. Ask yourself whether you see a future with him. If it doesn't seem right, don't entertain it any further.

The Becoming Woman

Five key questions to consider when courting are as follows:

1) **What's my first impression of him?** – what comes to mind when you see him? Do you focus on his physical appearance, job occupation, how he communicates, what his interests are?

2) **How well do you know him?** – Is the man you are looking to court a referral from a close friend? A primary or secondary school friend? Did you meet him online and read their profile to determine your decision?

3) **Is he gracious towards others?** – Monitor the way he speaks when you are around; how does he sound to the cashier or staff member at the till? Is he patient and kind or restless? – Does he speak positive words or are they negative? Does he speak well of his family and friends?

4) **Does he share the same values?** – What do you both have in common? Does he share the same faith? Do you like A and he likes B? Do you both eat similar foods?

5) **Can I trust him to keep his word?** – Is the man integral and committed to what he says? What have people said about him? Does he act as a trustworthy individual?

These questions are essential during the stages of courting and being mindful of where you stand in the relationship. This isn't about changing the man but allowing him to express himself in an organic and authentic way. We can't change people to be what we'd like them to be, but we can learn how to respond from their actions. Loving who you are will enable the man to be himself around you.

There's a tendency to have everything in order before *feeling* ready. This can include having your finances in check, healing from past traumas, and being comfortable with everyone around us, but we have to remember that everything won't always be perfect. Being able to build yourself up in the process is the starting point of attracting a healthy relationship. Notwithstanding, being mindful of your intentions for being in a relationship – are you the becoming woman who will add value to your partner's life or will you end up taking him for granted?

> **Two people won't always be perfect, but they will always strive to understand each other.**

Being in the courting season teaches us who we are as women; the strengths we possess, the weaknesses we face and how they work for our good. The ability to build an organic friendship starts with the following:

- *'What's your name?'*
- *'How are you doing today?'*
- *'It's nice to meet you!'*
- *'How did you find out about this event?'*

can be overlooked because of a deep focus for being in a relationship.

Other passive examples include:

- *'I like you because I believe you are the one for me; let's date NOW!!'...*
- *God told me you were the one in a dream...*

Ummmmm, have we forgotten manners? Don't allow desperation to force what isn't yet ripe! Where waiting seems like an enemy, the courting process prepares you for the next level; that special person isn't coming into your life to fill a void, but to add value. The man shouldn't be a liability to you but an asset. As a woman, you are also responsible for preparing yourself effectively prior to courting. When waiting, I decided to invest in myself with reading books which stimulated my mind and positioned me to get ready; these books strengthened, challenged and pruned me. I had to ensure that my mind was nurtured and fed with the right sources of encouragement and the perseverance to pursue purpose whilst believing that my time would come.

For those desiring to get married with purpose, I'd highly recommend a book called 'Not Yet Married' by Marshall Segal. A great and easy-to-read book! To share a brief snippet, the author emphasises on certain blessings that we can have only through patience. If patience isn't practised on a daily basis; it becomes easier to embrace instant gratification which eventually makes us forget how priceless and beautiful patience really is.

Whilst studying the book, my own courting process was in motion. I understood that it wasn't just about having the title of being in a relationship to my other half, but understanding who my first love is. To ensure that I was ready, God had to test me and make sure I wasn't putting my desires of being with a man over His Will.

The vision to only arrive at the destination doesn't allow you to embrace the first step of building an authentic friendship with the person you're interested in. Allow yourself to see what can be achieved when patience is in its rightful place, because nothing that is valuable will be wasted.

When it comes to knowing someone, see it as an interview session. When you apply for a job, it is important to read the description, ensuring that it aligns with what you desire and what the company expects from you when the they call you in for a meeting.

Once it fits with the vision you have in mind, you can take further action by doing research about the company, learning about its history, when it was founded, the purpose behind the company, its vision and mission statement etc. These steps form a healthy relationship and will be a great bonus when you are called in for the interview and proceed to the next stage.

Take the opportunity to write your personal experiences with courting. Whether it was or is your first time or you've been through several courting phases, how did it help with your growth and development, and what advice could you give to those who are expecting to be in the season of courting?

The Becoming Woman

Over to you: What did your initial courting process look like and what did you learn from it?

_____
_____
_____
_____
_____
_____
_____

> **The courting process is for mature people!**

We must also be mindful to remember that dating doesn't equate to courting, but leads up to the process of assessing whether the relationship is well-suited between a man and woman. When a man says he desires to date a woman, it doesn't automatically mean that both are compatible because they've only met once.

Dating can consist of speaking on the phone, receiving frequent texts, getting to know each other on a personal level, *dying to self* and being mindful of how much information is being shared whilst focusing on the maturity levels of your mental and emotional wellbeing. This will indicate the next steps of the courting process.

Questions that are difficult to discuss will take grace and patience to answer with ease. It will take time to open up about past experiences, whether they are sexual, verbal, addictive, emotional, family-oriented etc, however, these are the greatest moments for God to prepare you.

A man after God's own heart won't take advantage of a woman who has been sexually mishandled or mischievous in the past, however, he will use it to take her in, protect and keep her pure until marriage. The power of sex is effective in a marriage because it binds two people together. It is a covenant that one must honour and take seriously to avoid lustful thinking.

When lust occurs, it is because the mind is focused on what's in it for themselves. It's not about what society says, or whether they mock you because you're still a virgin. We all have a responsibility to look after ourselves, especially in these times and seasons to benefit our environments and influence our circle in the right way.

When the opportunity arises to ask such questions in dating, you are honest with your responses and wise on what to share. You have to be sensible and sensitive to the other person who is listening, and be open to what is being discussed. We are all broken vessels looking for wholeness, and that wholeness can only come from the One who made us uniquely.

If you can pass the test of being vulnerable in wisdom about past relationships, you will continue to pursue wisdom which leads to the next stage of building a genuine courtship. Building friendships in the dating stage is the greatest advice for everyone to take on board.

Just as two women build strong sisterhoods with one another, it also applies to building a friendship with the opposite sex. Doing it with ease and not using force indicates peace of mind and the ability to be yourself whilst respecting each other's perspectives.

These direct questions should bring clarity and an honest approach to where you are in the courting stage. When you open your mouth and speak what is on your heart, in wisdom, you will begin to receive what you've desired. I believe we all desire loyalty and respect, and for this reason, it comes with knowing what you can contribute in the relationship and not expecting it to be one sided.

Take the time to study and know the other person before signing the contract because God wants men to bear a greater responsibility for leadership and initiative in marriage, beginning with dating. This isn't to say women don't have a responsibility of ensuring she is prepared. The Becoming Woman ought to contribute to what she believes is in her capacity to do.

> **Remember that you aren't only marrying your best friend, you're marrying _into_ their family, their dynamics, their culture, their siblings, their mindsets, their patterns, their interests. It's a two-way street.**

At times, you may encounter moments where offense occurs, and for this reason, it is important to have self-control and discipline your words to know what to say at the right time. During the courting stages, there will be discussions that a man and woman may not agree on, which is to their own preference, nonetheless, it shouldn't open the door of disrespect because one isn't ready to share parts of their lives. Couples can learn about the beauty of agreeing to disagree in love, wisdom and humility.

You may have moments where you are looked at in a way that makes you question why you are single – for example, questions such as: 'You are doing very well in your career and have many accolades...so what's next in your agenda for settling down?' Others will be bluntly direct and ask where the other half is! When these pressuring moments come, remember that it takes a mature response to keep you on track.

Being silent doesn't equate to ignorance or rudeness, but it's getting to the stage where silence becomes a strategy of faith to build our patience levels. To be tempted in responding harshly for fear of being rejected doesn't make it easy to be found. As we get older and wiser, we understand the importance of having a gentle and quiet spirit which is attractive in a man's eyes (1 Peter 3:4).

Date in Private. Pray in Secret. Marry in Public.

Those you encounter whether on a daily or occasional basis won't always be willing to share their relationship status with others. We are all entitled to what we desire to share, and I believe that in wisdom, being led by the Holy Spirit will enable us to know when to speak and when to be silent. The beauty of spending quality time in God's Presence is to seek His perspective and the leading of confirmation.

The Becoming Woman

At a time where no one understood what was happening due to the Covid-19 pandemic, I decided to use that period to do a soul-search. I remember God placing in my heart to remember the gifts He invested in me including my writing skills, my eloquent speech, and how the business, Authentic Worth Publishing is dedicated to aspiring authors to use their stories and turn them into valuable books. At a time where it felt stagnant, God was birthing greatness in me.

During the pandemic, I was out of my comfort zone personally and professionally. Adapting to different needs and expectations whilst praying for answers to be confirmed took a while. I knew what was on my mind and how I desired to achieve them, however, I understood that it wasn't in my own strength. The beauty of that season was understanding in the moment I was right where God needed me to be – not knowing everything about my life and what tomorrow would bring.

Through consistent prayer and confirmation, I leaned into the voice of God and His style of communication. I surrendered my desires to Him, believing that He knew best (which He always does). To have a list of what you desire in the opposite sex isn't the problem, however, I made an intentional decision to encourage myself not to become obsessed with it. I wrote them down and left it without constantly going back and forth, and trusted that what was for me would be for me without the pressure of making it work according to my own timing.

There's no way I could afford being out of alignment due to my impatience in settling for just anyone. I knew and still know that God is writing my story and the purpose He has given me continues. I was wise enough to let go of what I had in mind to pursue God, my purpose and more importantly, my peace. I made the intentional decision to keep focusing on building Authentic Worth Publishing and the authors who needed further support in pursuing their writing goals.

2020 was my breakthrough year! God opened many doors and used pivotal moments to reveal what my prayers represented. Taking the leap of faith, I chose to listen carefully to the people He placed around me at the time; rather than questioning their responses, I told myself that God's Will should be done over mine.

The Becoming Woman

We know that God is the best match-maker, and of course, He chose the man who is ordained for me. In that period, I prayed, fasted, and eventually opened up to my family and a few friends about our courting. My fiancés relentlessness, kindness and intentions were and still are attractive. When he asked for my number, I wasn't too quick on giving it away, however, after a few weeks, I trusted God and eventually accepted it. The rest was history and we started communicating on a daily basis.

It's the beauty of communication and having open questions which sparked the flow. The courting process was a raw, yet exciting time – moments of speaking about the past, hard times, tears, vulnerable moments, to then sharing seasons of joy, achievements, celebrations and being open minded to what the future holds. Had I decided to stay in my feelings or make haste decisions, it wouldn't have turned out the way I'd expected.

I really want to emphasise the importance of communication because a lot of relationships, especially at the beginning and intermediate stages can shy away from it. I believe communication is what can save a relationship. When two people can be verbal and open about their thoughts on what's on their mind, it creates a sense of ease and peace within. When two people can share in honesty what is on their heart, it becomes easier to build trust and know them on a deeper level.

What others see on a surface level, two people are able to witness and experience on a deeper intimate level. The key is not to be afraid of what the other person may think or say with the aim to get your point across in wisdom, gentleness and understanding. We must be mindful that our perceptions of people may not always be presented in the way one would expect.

For example, you may assume that your decisions are exactly the same as your potential spouse, but realise he may have a different perspective because you didn't ask directly at the initial stage of courting. The courting process enables you to discuss visions, ideas, share struggles, celebrate happy moments and more importantly, be present with each other.

Fast forward to 2021, having made our intentions known and understanding the roles we both represent in our lives, the first step was submission – submitting was my peace in that I didn't have to figure out or try to fit the pieces in my head. I chose to release my faith, let go and enjoy the moment together. This included being able to go out on dates, meeting up with friends, an introduction to family, having healthy and meaningful discussions on the phone and being present with each other set everything in motion.

> **Wise counsel advises not to speak *prematurely*.**

This is not to say that you can't share your achievements and wins, but it is vital to remember that there is a right time and season for everything to be revealed. There will be times where God will expose you to shine and other times where God will protect you in the secret place. Either way, these seasons teach us how to remain humble, especially when God is blessing us in many dimensions.

It can be tempting to show off and let others see what God is doing in our lives, and if not carefully monitored, can end up being spiteful towards others. Nobody wakes up and says 'I want to be heartbroken' and for this reason, we must know what parts of our lives are hidden or shared with a faithful few.

For those who know me, I am the woman who doesn't speak without praying, neither do I talk in advance until the outcome is fulfilled. We can easily become accustomed with talking about the early stages which are to be the most private moments of a woman's journey in courting. You shouldn't be pressured to post your partner up just because others want to see how he looks, unless you are posting for the purpose to encourage and reflect Christ-like relationships.

The focus was on developing myself and working on my wellbeing. I wasn't rushing to be with just anyone; I knew that God had to be in the centre of every decision. As I continued praying, it was becoming more intentional for the man who was pursuing me at the time to ask me out for a date. Peace was at the forefront, and through his calm mannerisms, gentle aura and intentions, I gave the situation to the Lord and remembered promising myself that I will be open-minded in wisdom.

When my fiancé proposed in November 2022, I made an intentional decision to keep my relationship status private, until I

The Becoming Woman

sought God to confirm whether it was the right time to share. A few weeks later, my parents also celebrated their 40th wedding anniversary and was so exciting to witness! As the becoming woman on a journey, my thoughts and sensitivity came from the place of interceding for other women who were also waiting for their divine breakthroughs in being with their other half.

I am aware of the pressure, the tears behind closed doors and delays that some women have experienced. The decision to be around like-minded prayer warriors and those in the prophetic sphere helped the season of preparing and becoming. Being in a season of building yourself to the stage of courting takes reflection, grace and favour, and I must say that in order for God to reign down and grant your hearts desires, He has to trust you before releasing it.

At times, you will also witness couples who have courted for a couple of months, become engaged in the process and ultimately get married within a year or two; God knew that they were both ready. The length of being in a relationship is determined by the One who put two people together in the first place for God's ultimate purpose which is of high value and importance.

> **There is no timeline of the 'right time' to get married – when you draw closer to the Lord, He reveals the steps by working on your heart first. What you are getting into is a permanent commitment/covenant and must be taken seriously.**

Being in the courting stage is not an opportunity to flaunt or make other women jealous. The man God has given you is a gift to do life with, not to use as a way to boost your pride. Despite the pressures we see to be in a relationship at a specific age, it shouldn't make us jump into it without divine direction. The focus of being in the courting stage isn't only to plan a wedding, but to embrace a lifetime of long-lasting marriage afterwards.

We should be mindful not to take heed to what society says about how weddings should look like, forgetting that a lifetime of marriage is far more precious that a couple of hours celebrating the big day. In as much as wedding planning has been an intense,

The Becoming Woman

pleasant and exciting experience, I am mindful that it was only for a season. I am willing to embrace and enjoy marriage how it should be, learning more about myself, putting my needs aside and allowing my partner to have his say, and many other healthy balances that keep a relationship stable and active. A wise person should know that social media doesn't equate to what is happening in the reality of someone's life.

When the courting stage comes, it may not necessarily look like what you had envisioned, but it's worth the wait and being able to position yourself for what it will bring. The stretching, pruning and uncomfortable moments are to be cherished as it continues to resonate with you on your journey to becoming. Having read this chapter, how will it prepare you for the future courting process?

_____

_____

_____

_____

_____

_____

_____

The courting stage for me was not about the end-goal or focusing on how nice the dress was, how many bridesmaids I wanted or the number of guests present, but understanding what God wants me to fulfil for His Glory and knowing my partner more intimately.

I've been blessed to study the book 'Things I wish I'd known before we got married' by Gary Chapman during my engagement season. This book covers a broader spectrum of what it means to be in a secure relationship which requires an honest and upfront perspective and certain questions being asked before saying 'I do.' The book reminds readers not to just plan a wedding, but a stable marriage and to reap the rewards for preparing well.

I believe it's vital to have a community of couples who reflect the beauty of Christ and produce much fruit in their relationships.

The Becoming Woman

Surround yourself with like-minded people who are in the courting stages, and in wisdom, ask questions you believe are helpful. In maturity, you will receive the relevant answers and use them as you see fit.

The courting stage is about perseverance and the willingness to see life from another perspective; it's not about yourself, but the other person you're entertaining. When this becomes a priority, you will start to see the fruit of the courting phase increase and become stronger.

As Proverbs 14:1 reminds us that a wise woman who builds her home is to be praised, but a foolish woman who doesn't prepare to take responsibility tears it down with her own hands. Don't be a foolish woman; be the Becoming Woman.

Reflection: Whether you are dating, courting or engaged, you must examine the foundation of your relationship and learn the skills from courting to building a successful marriage!
#TheBecomingWoman.

Chapter S.I.X.
-
Money and Savings

"It starts with the numbers! Be financially wise and responsible to build for a better tomorrow."

Money, money, money! A valuable asset, but is it that much of a big deal in relationships? Some may see money as a love-hate relationship, particularly with the cost-of-living crisis becoming more imminent. The pressure is serious with prices shooting up for getting on the property ladder, paying higher taxes, planning a wedding, nurturing a family; all whilst trying to enjoy life! One of the most important questions you must be able to answer confidently is: "How good am I with money?" It's easy to focus on how much one would ideally like to earn, however, with what is being made, how much wisdom is being applied to sustain and multiply it?

When you receive money either from your job, your business or family/friend, what is your first step? Is it putting 10% in your savings account, growing your investment funds or spending it? During the courting stage, I understood the importance of not only levelling up mentally and emotionally, but also managing my finances well. In every stage of our lives, we must learn about investing, budgeting, saving and capitalising our finances. It is important to be real with where you are financially, cutting back on unnecessary spending.

I am a believer that it's not only vital to know how much you are earning, but using your earnings for expansion. We can end up complaining that we don't have enough money, or every time we get paid, bills are literally coming out left, right and centre. A friend and I had a good chat about the cost of living and were discussing the way workers weren't only paid well enough, but what they have left to live on. How would it extend to local charities, families, children, and generations?

The Becoming Woman

It's important to get to the root of the underlying problems which occur within our community and it starts with understanding the economy. Whether you work locally or abroad, workers who make a living from their jobs aren't the cause of being paid a minimum wage. It's up to the Governments to change their ways and find solutions to support their citizens.

For this reason, our millennial generation are discovering that their gifts and talents can be turned into profitable streams of income that are fruitful and purposeful towards their audience which can supplement their current salary. It will take a major mindset shift to get to the stage where you start seeing results from your gifts, and although it may take a while, the reality is that you've started and can continue.

Despite the financial hardships, it is important to acknowledge and work with what you have. It can be tempting to complain, and in a relationship, one may have their views on spending collectively or separately. Either way, we have to confront how we see money and have a better understanding of it. This is a vital stage to be discussed before the engagement season.

When two people come together and are intentional about the future and what they are looking to achieve, it creates room for transparency. It's not easy talking about ones' financial status and where they are with money, especially if they aren't familiar with speaking about it or may feel embarrassed about how much they're currently earning.

It will take a level of maturity to discuss openly where you are and find solutions to keep moving forwards. We hear a lot about generational wealth, and this brings me to The Priestly Blessings in Numbers 6:24-26 that God will surely bless and keep us and that our blessings will overflow to our children's children. It may be a mindset block, but it doesn't have to affect the way you view money, particularly when two people are building collectively. Even though times are challenging, it doesn't mean that life can't be enjoyed. We can't always hide from our fears of money.

I remember moments where I'd be so nervous looking at my bank balance and I know I'm not the only one! There are seasons in our lives where it will be difficult to admit when one is struggling, but it's another bondage not to speak out and share with someone what you are going through. You don't always have to be strong, but you have to be real.

> **Until you learn how to embrace your fears with money, you will never learn how to persevere and expand it.**

A wise woman knows how to save and invest her money. I love the Proverbs 31 woman because she doesn't settle; rather, she uses her gifts to keep pushing. I wasn't always good with savings as it's easy to dip in and out. Now, I see money as an exchange to serve the Kingdom, the community and my loved ones in the ways that I can, and this is not to say I've arrived. I am still on a journey and believe that God will grant knowledge and wisdom on how to multiply and impact future generations.

I remember joining an online course about business, finances and stewarding money wisely. I took a lot from the session and applied it into my own life during the courting stages. I understood the importance of saving and budgeting even when I was single and I encourage you to do the same. It's unwise to wait and assume that a man will do everything for you.

To all the ladies – you better bring value to the table! Yes, you are beautiful, but you are also responsible for stewarding your life. It isn't attractive for a woman to be a liability. Don't become a burden; rather, choose to invest in yourself by taking those extra classes, creating an online course to teach clients, and investing in other activities which are beneficial for your educational growth.

We have one life to live and we will enjoy it, nonetheless, if you budget correctly for social activities, you will be able to manage your finances in other areas too. It's easy to keep saying "One day when I make it…", but in Luke 16:10 it says "He who is faithful in every little thing is faithful also in much, and He who is dishonest and unjust in every little thing is dishonest and unjust in much." If you can't save £100 a month out of your salary, you won't be able to save £1,000 a month. Start gradually. Let us be wise with our spending.

The Becoming Woman

I am not ignorant to the fact that money is a useful tool for this side of life. Nonetheless, as a woman who is working towards destiny and purpose, the more you focus on your passion behind what you do, the easier it is for money to gravitate itself to you. My greatest moments of financial breakthroughs were when no pressure was placed on me to make a certain amount. I'd say 'unlimited funds are my portion' because giving a specific amount assumed that was all I was worth.

My worth isn't based on how much money I make, but allowing the One who gives me the power to make wealth to collaborate with Him and create generational prosperity for others to benefit from. Notwithstanding, goals are set in place for financial freedom, however, I am not allowing what I haven't yet achieved to weigh me down.

> **I am also mindful that what I earn or the amount of money in my account doesn't reflect my worth, who or how blessed I am.**

The words we speak are life or death, and when you are tempted to say a harsh word about your life and where you are financially, discipline your tongue because these attitudes are a reflection of character and how mature you'll be in handling money for the future. In addition, culture will categorise you according to how much money you make, causing you to feel unworthy, frustrated and eventually start cutting corners to make others happy.

When this happens, especially in a relationship, the pressure to make more money becomes a hassle; you start trying to work it out in your own strength. Don't allow yourself to be moved by status, but talk freely with your partner and discuss ways both of you can make life count.

Passion and purpose work together, so when you have a passion or hunger for change and growth, you have to create solutions to that problem. Opportunities will find you, invest in you and pay you for your expertise, which in turn is used to re-invest in those areas of development. Don't allow what God has blessed you with to be taken for granted because you are earning more than you imagined.

The Becoming Woman

Money can come speedily but it can also finish quickly as well. Nothing in life is stable, whether you have a successful business or working in a high-end corporate firm. In all things, be humble for no one knows what tomorrow will bring.

Due to the society we live in, we see couples that look great online, posting their lifestyles and showing highlights, but do we know what goes on behind closed doors? We don't know whether it could be a cover up to hide a deeper void. Let's not be deceived by what we see!

There is a thin line between being wealthy and being financially illiterate. You can give a wealthy man and the illiterate man the same amount of money to spend on whatever they like. The wealthy man may spend it on temporary items that won't benefit his future, whilst the illiterate man may invest because he understands what it is to lack the skill of multiplication.

When you appreciate the small, you will honour the bigger blessings. What you do with money at this present moment in time determines how financially stable you'll become in the near future and this applies in a relationship. Have you created a safe environment to talk about where you are on the financial ladder? Secondly, are you living up to the expectations of what you are desiring? Asking is the first step, but positioning yourself in a way that you are ready to attain your goals by taking action is the ultimate key.

Some women may be content in their season of financial stability. Whether earning a lot or not, they understand that joy isn't in their careers or business endeavours. Does that mean being eager for more is wrong? No, it isn't. When you put God first and seek His Will above yours, ask what you desire and it will be given onto you in reference to Matthew 6:33.

As becoming women, we must never let anything God gives us rob Him of being first in our lives. I believe that happiness isn't determined by what you own; it's focused on a relationship with God because every blessing flows from Him. God will give you values and priorities to live by. Happy is the woman who delights in doing His commands.

Financial breakthroughs will find you because you have decided to put God over your problem. Ladies, we all need money, whether that's to do our hair, our nails, go on holiday, take a break, to treat our friends and loved ones etc, but we ought to develop self-control. If not, money will control you. I remember in my early 20s, I'd say that when I attained a high paid job, I will enjoy my life. I created a lifestyle that made me work tirelessly, and that sis, is not the soft life at all!

When we see women aiming high and getting where they need to be, we tend to get envious thinking how they excelled so quickly and why nothing has changed for us. You eventually look down on yourself and start to compare your life with those around you, and in turn, start losing hope. This is what causes you to work in your own strength and spend excess money that could've been invested for the future.

You assume that money will give you respect or attention, when really, it's made you more desperate and in turn, causing you to compare your reality to another person's relationship. What you see in ones' relationship shouldn't deter you from what God has promised you. Stay humble and appreciate who you are whilst embracing being financially content.

No matter how eager you are to be in a relationship, it's important to have a positive mindset about money. From a single perspective, the lifestyle is essential and easier to enjoy; you can travel anytime, eat out, save and ultimately be in control of how your finances grow through investments and other means of financial wellness.

For couples, one would need to be cautious about the way money is spent, especially when tying the knot because it's not 'his money' or 'her money' but 'our money' – a partnership. There are relationships which prefer having their money separate and is their own choice. Nonetheless, for the purpose of peace, trust and transparency in the home, working together has to be taken into account.

In the courting process, it's important to be mindful of your own financial status where you are responsible for the income, expenses, savings and purchasing habits. Secondly, your partner's financial status is also paramount to see how both can work collectively well. It is important to remember that not having 'enough' money shouldn't stop you from pursuing a relationship. This has been a hard truth for some and has made it difficult to be real for fear of losing a loved one, or being in debt and not finding a way to pay it off.

The Becoming Woman

Be honest with where you are and ask yourself whether it's your priority to be financially independent, but don't stay silent about it. We have to remember that it's not just about the ring and how much it's worth, but also how much money you'll have after the wedding is finished. What have you got set in place, whether from the man, the woman, or both? It is important to be mindful that as a single person, you are responsible for your finances.

Now that two are becoming one, there is a shared collective. As long as both parties are doing what they believe deems to be successful financially, working and communicating are key tools for improving financial knowledge and the ability to have a well-balanced and healthy marriage.

One of the most challenging moments in 2018 was when my sister passed away, and for that reason, I was very intentional about seeking God for the next steps on how to continue the legacy of her life. This also included me being honest about where I was at the time and the focus on understanding the property process. Having lived with my parents, it taught me how to mentally and practically support and prepare for adulthood, being responsible with my finances, and at the same time, making the most of it with my family.

I can't thank God enough for my family, and whether you are reading this book and eager to leave home, take your time and ask yourself what is the purpose.

God exceeded my expectations and I chose to stay where He needed me to be, although it was nice to live with family during my single season. However, what is good for one isn't good for the other. I want to put emphasis on this that even if you are in your 30s and living with your family, don't ever be ashamed. Society isn't going to build your life and what others say isn't valid, neither are they going to pay your mortgage! Stay true to who you are and wait. God will come through for you. He did it for me.

Pursuing purpose and leaving my previous job was a big leap of faith. The opportunities that've been given and the amazing people I've met and continue to meet keeps me going. Having a supportive man is a bonus and this is because waiting was in the mix. Had I become restless and thought of my own way, I don't believe this book would've been written, let alone transitioning from relying on a job to fully depending on God with the creative skills to bring innovative ideas and solutions to the community.

The Becoming Woman

Regardless of the waiting season, I pressed through and persevered, and ultimately, God exceeded my expectations and for that, I am grateful. My fiancé is a relentless man who knows what he wants. As we were discussing, it gave me calmness as we continued our plans and was more evident that he was serious about wanting to be with me.

I needed to change my mindset about money and rather than being pressured to perform, I was able to be myself and learn from his mindset to build a life together. When you are trusting God to be in a relationship, it's not about having everything in your life fall in place, because broken parts can still be mended.

My beautiful sister Keeley says that **"Broken crayons still colour."** Everyone's life has meaning; despite where you are right now, it can be beautiful. You will know the right time to talk about a situation in your life which can also be revealed through a loved one who is praying for you.

Whether you or your partner is working full time and the other is running a business, it can still work, although both parties must come to a mutual agreement on the next steps. It may be a stretch at times, but when you are not expecting one person to do everything, it enhances the relationship. "Is there anything you'd like me to support you with?" is a great question to ask your husband to be.

Society deems it fit to allow the man to do everything, but seasons are changing; women can also treat their partners and support what they are working hard for regarding the family. There has to be balance, structure and integrity when coming to the stage of agreement.

Being in a relationship isn't an easy task; we don't want to glamourise and forget there is life behind social media. Couples who are looking to serve with the intention to uplift one another will find alternative means to work it out. That's the beauty of perseverance; when one is discouraged, the other should speak life. We have to learn from our past spending habits, focus on how we are currently spending and plan for a better tomorrow. Although there are many resources and books on how to manage money and increase savings, start with where you are. Be truthful and honest about what you want to improve in your financial journey as this is a vital component in any relationship.

The Becoming Woman

> **Having a great vision starts with the gradual steps and where you currently are. Don't forfeit the process.**

Ultimately, be mindful of your spending habits and know what and where you are putting your finances into. Giving is about sacrifice and this is what makes a relationship fruitful. Start off with reassuring your spouse that you are working on building financial stability and this will eventually open opportunities that wouldn't have been known had our mouths been quiet about money.

Reflection: In all circumstances, look for the good in everything and be thankful. Analyse your spending habits and be honest with how you use your finances. No matter what you have, make it work and allow it to build and strengthen your relationship! *#TheBecomingWoman.*

Chapter S.E.V.E.N.

-

Love or Lust?

"The mind is the battlefield."

In my early 20's, I had a deep desire to develop my relationship with God and began studying the topic of love. I had an understanding that God loved me, but needed a greater revelation. Love is a powerful force which takes us through the most difficult trials with the intention to remember that His Presence resides with us at all times. The challenges we may have about love is the longevity, generosity and sustainability of it. Thoughts can consist of the following:

- Will I mess this up?
- Is this going to last?
- Am I allowing fear to stop me from opening my heart?
- Will this person stay in my life forever?
- Am I ready to fully commit, or do I just want him for comfort?

When we doubt God's love, it's because we haven't yet tapped into His unconditional love for us. We become so caught up in man's love and use our strength to fill the voids that we forget before man, God appeared first.

The lust of what we see on social media or how much money we can make is more delightful than the One who gave us life on the Cross. No matter how far life has taken you, everyone is built for love. No one should assume they can be successful on their own, neither should there be any intention to lust over what may not last.

It's easy to lust over someone you've had an eye on. I couldn't stop thinking about this guy I *'fell* in love' with in my 20's. Initially, I wasn't interested in him, but what I admired was his persistence and decided to give it a go. As time went on, we exchanged numbers and got to know each other.

The Becoming Woman

The discernment of seeing that he wasn't ready for a committed relationship made me step back and not force anything to happen. I let it flow naturally and eventually, we kept it calm and decided to stay as friends. In the end, I felt empty because my flesh kept telling me he was the one, but my Spirit was saying that God had someone much better for me.

Time is a gift that when used wisely adds value, but when misused, it adds further delays. It is important to invest your time in someone who shows the same level of interest and more. If you don't learn how to manage your time and emotions, it will distract you from your purpose and cause the wrong attention to gravitate towards you. We may not always know what our purpose is straight away, but as each day goes by, life's experiences will shape us to see where we're positioned.

I assure you becoming woman; the love God has for you comes with His best intentions in mind. God gives inner peace and a lightness in every moment. We ought to understand and rest in the fact that not having a physical companion doesn't equate to being unloved, but the man who seeks God earnestly is the man God is reserving for you. Whilst you are enjoying your life, the man God has for you is also enjoying his, and at the appointed time, He will bring you both together for a purpose.

As you grow in spiritual maturity and wisdom, it is important to cherish and celebrate people who come into your life. You don't only honour people for what they have, but who they are and their existence. When you start dating because of how someone looks or how much money they have, eventually, the person will realise this and step away. No one wants to be taken advantage of because we are all precious. Remember that lust isn't only sexual, it can be material-based as well. Being with someone for the benefits and not to invest in their wellbeing journey is detrimental to your progress as an individual.

You can purposefully position your mindset to be intentional about your thoughts and words before making any commitment to being with someone. Your character reflects the person you desire to be with, so ensure you take the time to not only study his accolades, but focus on his behaviour and mannerisms and be honest with yourself. It is important to take time and invest in personal growth when it comes to character-building and analysing our thought-patterns.

Are we impatient during the process which opens up the door to lust, or do we selflessly allow the other person to make their own choices whilst respecting them? There may be a tendency to control and focus on what we desire to see without taking into consideration two people who make a decision from different perspectives.

When sharing your opinions or perspectives, the first question to ask yourself is 'what's the motive?' – when this is clear, it makes it easier to differentiate love vs lust. Responding from a place of love requires gentleness, patience and the commitment to understand one another, whereas lust entertains a self-minded attitude and fixation of the outcome that suits one person over the other. We must learn to adopt the beauty of having healthy communication to build relationships as a vital component to a strong union.

> **Your character is being developed when you choose to love and run away from the lust of the world.**

According to the late Dr. Myles Monroe, he stated in one of his relationship seminars *three tests* which influences the characteristics of love or lust which include the following:

1) **Power** – Power isn't always about title, positions and accolades. It's how you handle people when you reach another level and treating others. As women, we must be very mindful that the lust of a man's physical appearance, what he drives, or how he dresses doesn't become the contributing factors to choosing him. When you have power, you can use it to your own advantage or detriment. An individual operating in discernment will understand when to open up or when it's time to leave. Power defines character, and when it is out of alignment, it will eventually be misused. The more power you gain, humility must follow.

2) **Money** – This tool is a healthy indicating factor for the progression stages in a relationship. As discussed in chapter 6, savings and handling money are great signs of growth, ease of mind and wisdom in being able to multiply. When you lust after money or complain that you don't have enough, it becomes easier to withhold it, spend recklessly and allow pride to let others know how much you are earning due to competition. No matter how much you are earning, it doesn't make you superior than those who earn less. There may be moments where a man earns less money but has a calm pleasant life as he appreciates the fact that little is better than nothing, whilst another man who earns twice as much doesn't have peace and is likely to mismanage what he's earning. When money is used in an unhealthy manner, it brings up different forms of inappropriate behaviour. Don't let this be you. It's an honour to be trusted not only to make wealth, but to give to others and be responsible for the return on investment.

3) **Sex** – A gift that God gave a man and a woman is sex; to be fruitful, intimate and multiply in reference to Genesis 1:28 and take dominion over the earth. In marriage, sex is pleasurable because it not only honours your spouse's body, but also honours God. When sex is misused and causes one to lust and start disrespecting your body, it becomes easier for others to follow suit. A man who loves you and loves God will not lust over a woman's body. He will wait for you. He knows that it is a great responsibility to protect and honour the woman he claims to love.

In the message (MSG) version of 1 John 2:15-17 it says that we should not love the world's ways. Yes, we are in the world, but we don't have to love the world's goods. Love of the world squeezes out love for the Father. In essence, everything that goes on in the world including wanting your own way and to appear important has nothing to do with the Father. The world and all its cravings won't last, but whoever does what God desires is set for eternity. It will take the strength of God to keep you grounded in Him and focus your gaze on what makes Him glad.

The Becoming Woman

Before you commit to the relationship, is your heart free from lustful desires of the past? Can you resonate with situations that people go through, and how do you apply love to support them on their journey? Remember there are people who understand your journey and have seen you cry when you were broken. They were present when life was tough and had a breakdown. Cherish those people who stand with you during the hard times and allow them to remind you of joy, peace and harmony. In essence to this, we must learn how to support and work with each other, especially when they are dealing with painful situations that can't always be expressed in words.

Let's be transparent: write about a time where you were crushed to the point where you broke down and removed yourself away from others. Was it a breakup? Was it low self-esteem? How did this impact your relationship with love vs lust and what did the season teach you?

_____

_____

_____

_____

_____

_____

As women, our natural tendencies are to hide or numb the pain by isolating ourselves, choosing not to be sociable and avoiding several questions being asked. Yes, you may still be going through the painful moment of the heartbreak or the loss of a loved one, nonetheless, we choose to advance from the pain one step at a time. No matter how long it takes, the process matters and can't be skipped especially during the transformation and healing stages. The moments we choose to be still and allow the season to change our hearts will eliminate lust and bring in the aura of love.

The Becoming Woman

Love each other and develop deeper bonds with your sisters and friends. The beauty of sisterhood and their singleness is when they are able to intercede and pray for one another. It doesn't cost to ask your friend what they'd like prayers for especially when you've noticed they've been quiet for a while. Don't be obsessed with getting your own advantage. Forget yourselves long enough to lend a helping hand, especially when you sense God is moving mightily in your life. When you are at the brink of a breakthrough, the next focus is to remind others that God is able!

There's a beautiful aura when we don't know what to do. At times, we assume our answers are the best, but truly, we are lost without His direction. Think of yourselves the way Christ Jesus thought of Himself. Jesus; although He had equal status with God didn't think so much of Himself. When the time came, Jesus set aside the privileges of deity and took on the status of a slave and became human and didn't claim any special privileges. Now that is power!

To die to self is not only self-sacrificing, but it brings honour. The love that we should develop for others should be a constant determination to overcome the spirit of lust and emulate love. Even the times where your prayers aren't being answered will challenge you to trust God that He is working all things out for your good.

It may feel good for a short while to have public praise, but in the end, it leads to loneliness and a heart full of sorrow. You don't want to give birth to lust because of pride or not taking into account your errors and faults to receive correction.

I've learnt the one-two second rule when another person is communicating, and this is very important not only in sisterhood, but in a potential relationship to give space and time to receive a response. I am still on a journey and currently loving it. Each day, there is always a lesson to learn about yourself and the environments you are surrounded with. I enjoy the beauty of dialogue and taking the time to pause before responding and listening.

A man of good character, integrity and intentions isn't only focusing on a woman's appearance, but how willing they are to adapt to each other. I enjoy having deep conversations that enable me to change not only my perspective, but help me to see observations from another person's point of view which doesn't lead to disagreements or bitterness.

The Becoming Woman

God has been faithful through the transition of singlehood to being a fiancé and soon to be wife. I have seen the growth stages in my life that has been mixed with tears, perseverance and relentless faith. It has taken me consistency to build my life at the stage I am and continue to use my experiences to encourage others who may be feeling left behind. I know it's easy to have thoughts of how much you'd like to achieve and live a comfortable life, but do you know there is beauty when plans don't always go your way? I've realised when doing my part in faith and believing it will work in my favour, that is where I am able to embrace peace and relax.

A man and woman planning the next stages of marriage may come with some agreements and disagreements, but the beauty about this process is to embrace each other's differences and not look elsewhere because of boredom and frustration. The power of lust and love in a relationship will either help the two grow together or forfeit it. How willing are you to keep the love alive and refuse to entertain signs of lust?

> **Lusting over someone because of what they have brings dissatisfaction which causes you to obtain what you can't maintain.**

As mentioned previously, lust is a slow detrimental indicator that leads to manipulative behaviour which eventually benefits one person over the other. We have to be mindful and wise to ensure these behaviours are identified and caught out before committing to the next stage of the relationship process. Having studied James 4:13-17, it teaches and warns us about not being too ahead of ourselves and plan with wisdom. To simplify it with a potential relationship, let's look at the following verses individually in James 4:13-17 (ESV); it reads:

(13) Come now you who say, "Today or tomorrow we will go into such and such a town and spend a year there and trade and make a profit." – Scenario 1: a man may approach a woman with no motive for the future, other than to make money and live the good

The Becoming Woman

life. There hasn't been a time where both the man or woman speaks about purpose and what they've been called to do because it's about what they both can gain.

(14) "Yet, you do not know what tomorrow will bring. What is your life? For you are a mist that appears for a little time and then vanishes!" – Scenario 2: being unprepared is the result of love and lust being mixed together. Your life is precious, so ensure that you live it out to the best of God's ability. Everything you do on earth will be remembered, therefore, your legacy matters.

(15) Instead, you ought to say, "If the Lord wills, we will live and do this or that." – Those who want to attain higher levels must learn how to stay grounded and submit. Being grounded doesn't mean you are hidden; it means you are willing to be stretched through the submission process, allowing the Holy Spirit to guide and lead you to the right direction causing lust to cease and love to increase.

(16) "As it is, you boast in your arrogance. All such boasting is evil." – Due to the intensity of the workload and what has been achieved throughout the process, it may not look like pride when you are talking about a few accolades, but when you start comparing your success with others to give yourself a greater name, that is arrogance. For this reason, relationships can only go so far. You must learn to live in harmony and honour each other with words of wisdom, not harsh or damaging competition.

(17) "So, whoever knows the right thing to do and fails to do it, for him it is sin." – When an instruction is given to you, how quickly do you take it on board? Don't be like the man who looks at himself in the mirror and when he goes away, doesn't even remember what he looks like. *Reference scripture: James 1:23.*

It will take the Grace of God to help us abstain from anything that will trigger or bring chaos in the future to a marriage, especially when you have blind spots you aren't aware of. We know that building a relationship isn't a smooth process as it comes with sensitive moments due to family dynamics, past traumas, and unresolved conflict.

The Becoming Woman

When it comes to love, it requires two people sacrificing their time with God and seeking a deeper revelation about who they are in Him. Our identity shouldn't be tied to someone else but to the Father who knows what we can handle. In turn, this will help us grow and understand how to love others and stand in the gap regarding ones' weaknesses.

Transitioning from the beauty of singlehood to courting is about listening, connecting and acknowledging where the other person is coming from. To the becoming woman; maybe you wanted the tall, dark and handsome man, but could this be an idol you've created for yourself that's causing you to miss out on other opportunities?

God doesn't view life the way we do; His ways are not our ways and His thoughts are not our thoughts (Isaiah 55:8). This is what should keep us mindful of how He is moving in our lives. We must learn how to be humble and come across in a pleasant manner. Just as words are soothing to the soul, it brings joy to a great relationship; the same way harsh words crush a potential relationship.

As we continue living on this side of life, there is a lot to glean from, but more importantly, being able to place healthy boundaries on how we allow lust into our lives. When God blesses you with a man who is intentional about you, it will take wisdom, grace and self-control not to entertain thoughts of pre-marital sex. It is possible to respect each other and wait until the appointed time to become intimate rather than entertaining lust in your heart. Our bodies have been purchased with a price and can't be misused anyhow.

Whether you've been sexually active in the past, as the becoming woman, you need to lean on God for strength to break this pattern when going into your next relationship. Notwithstanding, the man God has for you will ensure you are crowned and protected because the value he sees in you is worth waiting for. This is why *love* and *lust* are always in battle because it takes one to surrender and the other to dominate.

In turn, God honours you and your body because He created it in His own image. Allowing yourself to feel vulnerable to gain attraction or feel loved may not only be a put-off to some men, but it's distracting for your spirit.

To be engaged with who you are, especially as a woman who is becoming and evolving, we are responsible for how we treat

The Becoming Woman

ourselves. From the food we consume to the products we use on our skin.

In 1 Peter 3:3, Apostle Peter emphasises on our beauty not coming from the outward adornment such as elaborate hairstyles, wearing gold jewellery or fine clothes. Now, some may oppose to this and think why can't we look good? It's very important to look good, but what keeps lust out is looking good in moderation and not overdoing it.

You don't need what you think you're missing out on. Humility has a massive part to play, especially when you know your financial and emotional levels. If you can't afford it, it's okay. Everyone has been through these stages; however, it is important to make sure you don't lose sleep and keep your mind, body and soul healthy so that fruitful relationships with yourself and others will emerge.

In essence, lust isn't just focusing on ones' body, but is anything that distracts you from your purpose.

From a relationship perspective, we must learn how to place healthy boundaries with our potential spouse and those who come our way. Giving each other space enables us to process our thoughts individually. When love is real, lust breaks and eventually, you are able to heal from past situations.

Your weaknesses shouldn't push you to lustful thoughts by questioning who you are because the waiting season is taking a while. The season is helping you work on loving yourself. Ultimately, self-control matters and when you are able to pass the test, you will learn how to strengthen others to overcome lust and replace it with genuine love.

Reflection: No matter how much you desire commitment, reciprocation and love, all these can happen effectively if you die to yourself and focus on how to become a better woman and avoid entertaining what will cost you in the future.
#TheBecomingWoman.

Chapter E.I.G.H.T.
-
The Becoming Gentleman

"Calm, <u>gentle</u>, humble and intentional."

The becoming gentleman – a man who is on a journey is not only attractive, but desirable. There are differing views from society where they have thoughts of what a man should be and look like:

"He has to be aggressive because that's what shows masculinity!"

or

"He better pay for everything and contribute to our welfare!"

This is what some people assume and it makes me wonder what the foundation of the relationship will be in the future. For a successful relationship, a man is to invest his time in his identity and purpose to discern who his help-meet is. If you've reached this far on the book, well done and congratulations!

By permission, I've asked four men in different stages of life (married and not yet married) who share their perspectives on what it is to be a becoming gentleman in society, dating, marriage and most importantly, being themselves. Let's read what they have to say:

Becoming gentleman 1: Being a gentleman in today's society is slowly becoming under-appreciated. Whilst some expect it, others just don't value it at all. However, I am me; a unique individual who tailors his approach according to the babe. Being a gentleman is very easy; it's values which have been instilled in me from young. Whether it be ensuring she walks on the inside, or making sure she enters the door before I drive off is all part of what I believe a gentleman should be. Whilst chivalry is slowly becoming a dying artform, I would encourage my fellow men to continue. In short, the becoming gentleman is being masculine whilst having the ability to be gentle, kind and warm. We must make decisions and ensure our word is bond. Once this is achieved, we too can see positive changes in our society – *Anonymous.*

Becoming gentleman 2: In this day and age of 2023, becoming a gentleman has somewhat got harder when relating to the dating scene. My belief stems from the majority of individuals who have developed trust-issues from their past relationship(s) and/or the expectations a group of women may have prevented men from becoming their true self. We've known or heard of a toxic relationship or a bad break-up. We also know the effects that a toxic relationship can cause to either party (men and women). This can more times be the reason that becoming a gentleman in our society and the dating scene, whilst being yourself can be hard.

Becoming a gentleman can be looked at from two perspectives which are:

1) What you carry *within*; (Mannerism, integrity etc)
2) What you carry *without*; (Well-groomed, hard-worker etc)

The expectation can be highly demanding (in this fast-paced lifestyle) that we tend to portray ourselves in a different light which can at times pressurise the 'gentle' in the word gentleman. Those that know who they are in themselves do not tend to be phased by this, but on the contrary, others do. I strongly believe the quote that "you attract what you are and not what you want." Speaking on my personal journey, I have never managed to attract a toxic relationship in my life, nor a significant other with high demands that surpasses what I can offer. This has graced me with becoming a gentleman in my dating relationship. With that being said, if you find yourself not being who you are, this can be resolved by focusing on your internal-self first, whether it's healing and letting go of a past relationship to then work and attract the necessities outwardly. Yours Sincerely – *Anonymous.*

Becoming gentleman 3: Becoming a gentleman in our modern society requires a conscious effort to resist the negative influences from social media and the values adopted by the masses. It's a battle, but identifying positive role models and learning from them can help one stick to their values. In the dating/courting scene, being a gentleman means treating women with respect, courtesy, and kindness. It involves being attentive to their needs, showing interest in their lives, and being a good listener. These qualities can set you apart from others who may be more interested in superficial qualities.

When it comes to marriage, preparation is key. Before getting married, it's important to have enough self-awareness to know yourself, your purpose, and improve your faith and relationship with God. This process of self-discovery can help you be a better partner and build a stronger, more meaningful relationship. Finally, being yourself is essential to being a true gentleman. It's important to have a curious mindset and the trait of questioning things to understand why they are done in a certain way. Once you have found your identity, you can boldly walk in your truth of being a gentleman.

In summary, being a becoming gentleman in our society requires a conscious effort to resist negative influences, identifying positive role models, treating women with respect and kindness, preparing yourself for marriage, and being true to yourself – *Anonymous.*

Becoming gentleman 4: Being a gentleman is a behavioural attribute that is perceived to be acceptable, admirable and inspirational. A gentleman in such a sense would be a role model at

The Becoming Woman

work, home and the communities they are a part of. With this brief background, I would like to start with being a gentleman in our society and community today. This would mean being honest, truthful, law-abiding, having high moral values, diligent, decent, humble and empathetic. Such a man would need to maintain these values which ultimately leads to the overall package called integrity when practiced consistently overtime.

I do understand that challenges and temptations will always attempt to make one break or drop some of these values. This is why it takes a strong sense of determination, and for me, guidance from the Holy Scriptures to keep practicing and maintaining these values. In being a true gentleman, it requires strong spiritual values. Being a gentleman in the marriage scene requires additional attributes to the above-mentioned qualities.

The added requirements are to be loving, gentle, faithful to his wife, being a hard worker and provider, being a protector and one who nurtures the gift of his wife giving her freedom to grow in her gifts and talents. It means being a present father who inspires and is a role model to their children. Of course, as the head and authority in the home, such a man ensures discipline so the children are brought up with acceptable, moral and behavioural qualities in society.

Finally, as a becoming gentleman, it means being content with the blessings I have received. I don't try to be like someone else or envy another man; this ensures I don't enter the competition mode and have satisfaction and peace in that sense. I live each day with the understanding of the brevity of life and prioritise what really matters which is to love, be decent, share and be humble. In essence, to trust the Lord for the very best He has for me and always be thankful – *Anonymous.*

A man's intentions for you must come from a place of purity and generosity. The becoming gentleman is in the word itself; he is *gentle*. He speaks when relevant and knows when to be silent. A

The Becoming Woman

gentleman is a visionary who plans ahead for his future family. He takes intentional steps to not only work on himself, but is a hunter for the woman he intends to be with. I really enjoy writing about the becoming gentleman because it's not as if he's arrived and has it all together, but is learning each day how to pivot, innovate and bring solutions to the table.

He has a mindset of growth and is a risk-taker. He knows how to work smart and still have a balanced work/life. When you come across the becoming gentleman, learn to appreciate and embrace who he is. You may meet a man that may not necessarily fit your list, but eventually, you'll realise that what matters is the character being developed within.

Having read Touré Roberts book; Wholeness, a quote that's mentioned says:

> "Make sure you are just as beautiful on the inside as you are on the outside."

This doesn't only apply to men, but women too. Working internally is what brings about a healthy perspective. A confident individual is someone who is worth going after and investing time in. Society has made it seem that looking good outwardly without taking into account the inward accountability makes one neglect their mental wellbeing at the detriment of keeping up with societal trends.

As I learn each day in many ways, I take the time to pause, reflect and ask myself how I'd want to be remembered. It is important to prepare for these questions internally with the aim to work on the vulnerable areas that cause us to hide and cover it with excess spending and going over what we earn to try and get little-to-no attention in return.

Whatever takes you out of alignment will never be worth your life. It may not always be easy to identify the becoming gentleman due to the increasing pressure of society and how we desire our potential spouses to look like, let alone treat us. As women, we have our standards and expectations of what we deem as vital when a man is on the lookout.

The Becoming Woman

These can include the following:

They <u>must</u> be fine like wine!
They <u>must</u> be working at a very high paid job or have a successful business!
They <u>must</u> have their own property!
They <u>must</u> be driving!
They <u>must</u> be fit!
They <u>must</u> be taller than me! I am not dating any man who is short!

Does any of these statements resonate with you? If that's you, thank you for acknowledging it. Notice the word 'must' are all underlined. This is the demand we subconsciously give ourselves to make sure our needs are met. As a woman who is intentional about being in a relationship, be mindful that the pressure to perform what you need can cause friction between you both.

We should appreciate what the becoming gentleman can provide and the level of his work ethic, not indirectly comparing him to others or expecting him to have it all together. This can trigger a man's self-esteem, and if not careful, you lose the opportunity of having a great man that was meant for you and judging him too soon based on your preconceived ideas.

You may look back and in the long-run ask yourself was it worth all the pressure and hype to impress others for what they will define us as? This is a negative mindset to have, and giving yourself to fear of what people say or what you should do can break a solid relationship between a man and woman.

The becoming gentleman's need is to be appreciated and respected by a woman. Once this is out of place and becomes dominating, it will eventually grow unhealthy patterns of hurt especially if not dealt with from the past.

Notwithstanding, the becoming gentleman may have his own desires for the woman he intends to be with. The focus of this chapter is to remember the word *becoming*. Don't forget that in as much as you desire your potential spouse to have it all together, you also need to make sure you've got your life together as well, because it is a process. We can't be one-sided, neither can we disrespect the way someone looks for not being up to 'our standard.'

The Becoming Woman

Sis, do you remember that long list of desires you wanted in a man? You may have to limit some of them and let God in your heart. In the season of my singleness, I remember encouraging myself to be open minded and till today, it continues. I enjoy encouraging my sisters and friends to be open-minded and *wise*. What you see isn't with our physical eyes, but to gain spiritual discernment and insight on what truly matters. The beauty of the becoming man and woman is their work in harmony, not demanding that one should change to please the other.

> **It's been said a woman marries a man to change him, but a man marries a woman hoping she'll never change - Albert Einstein.**

He carries himself well; he is a lover of people, he shows compassion, he is strong and is a prayer warrior. You will look past the physical because you will be more in love with what's on the inside of the becoming gentleman. Seeking to desire companionship is about evolving and changing your perspective. When you think you know what it is to be in a committed relationship, you will truly discover another area about yourself that may need adjusting to ensure the union is balanced.

This requires you to be non-judgemental, especially when you've met for the first time. We must learn how to be gracious and humble enough to listen attentively to their story before we suggest what they should do.

It's listening to a story which brings humility and understanding. This is such a beautiful character trait to give someone else the opportunity of speaking without interruption. We shouldn't entertain judging others at the expense of trying to get even or ruling it over them, but taking the time to reflect and find ways to advance.

This stage will require a woman who is *patient*, loving, supportive, and kind. If these fruits aren't embedded in your own lifestyle, focus on embracing the single season until you are trusted to be in a committed relationship.

The Becoming Woman

When you are patient with your spouse, he will return the favour and be patient with you. The aggression or lack of love you feel from your partner doesn't necessarily equate to him not loving you; there will be moments where the becoming gentleman needs space to process his thoughts, especially when he sees a future with the woman he desires to be with. He doesn't want to rush the season of discovery, and therefore, lose the opportunity of having a great woman due to anxiety or lack of confidence.

Another perspective to be mindful of is the influence of our loved ones, particularly family members and close confidants. As a becoming woman, it's easy to be in environments where others want to see progress on a quicker scale.

Whether that's your immediate family, close relatives, good friends etc, the becoming gentleman also needs time to process his new season, and develop more of an intimate relationship with the woman's family. It's a beautiful commitment seeing a father-in-law and son-in-law get along very well. Let's be mindful, however, not to rush the process of the next stage, and take the time to enjoy the season of becoming – knowing the person intimately for who they are.

To add on this, being able to identify areas in your life that ought to be developed is important and shows you are ready for the next dimension of the relationship. Loving who you are matters greatly which impacts the way others view you. As a man who is intentional about pursuing a woman, he is already confident and well-informed by his own instincts that decisions are made solely from a healthy place and not desperation. Likewise, the becoming woman will wait patiently because she is already aware of the man's intentions and isn't influenced by her surroundings.

It's important to note that as a becoming gentleman, you are aware of her strengths and weaknesses, and ought to protect her by reassuring that everything is working in their favour. Leaving her at suspense to allow input from external environments can cause confusion which leads to lack of trust and over-analysing. Your peace is expensive and being in the season of choosing between two people must be dealt with utmost respect and integrity.

Proverbs 18:22 reminds us that when the gentleman finds a good wife, he has found a good thing and obtains favour from the Lord. The man leads the wife into a good home, safety and an open space

The Becoming Woman

to be honest, real and her authentic self. The becoming gentleman takes initiative to ensure that their relationship is based on God's Word and not internal or external influences of others.

A man of integrity, mannerisms and a positive work ethic will wait for his woman. He is confident the two will become one.

You don't have to be perfect, but you have to be willing. You are in the right season and God is constantly working on you, allowing your life to transform and show what is in you. Even when the pressure is there to perform and settle down quickly, He is crushing your pride, removing distractions and replacing them with a heart of new beginnings and gratitude.

I believe these are areas many young women struggle with because we tend to operate in our feelings which give off false perceptions misguiding the truth and creating images in our minds on how life should be. In those cases, God has a way of cutting our desires off before it grows into someone or something we may regret.

When the Bible talks about a Godly man, He is referring to the inner-man, not only the outward appearance. A man with good character, morals and a pure heart is so precious, valuable and rare. As a woman, desire the man who is becoming. He is becoming the mature, responsible and charming asset. Let him be and in turn, allow him to show you his own perspective of love and commitment.

In Ephesians 5:22, Apostle Paul encourages wives to submit to their own husbands as to the Lord. As mentioned in chapter 5 about the courting process, what are you learning about yourself that can be improved? You ought to submit and give your undivided attention to the man who comes your way as a sign of respect and honour not only to him, but onto God. Remember that as you submit to your husband, you are also allowing God to minister to him which will reap abundant fruit in the relationship.

There is a saying that 'behind every successful man is a woman'; a great man has a great woman by her side. A woman who suggests

The Becoming Woman

but is open-minded to allow the man to make decisions is a positive attribute to *mutual agreement* and sanity, however, it will still require greater responsibility for the becoming gentleman to lead the home. Being in a relationship shouldn't be difficult. Instead, we must let each person unfold naturally in their own way.

Trying to make suggestions on how the becoming gentleman should behave may restrict him from being his best self, rather; he desires to embrace a life of his own, to walk in who he is and be who God intends for him.

The man who is after God's heart is committed to knowing Him and will likely emulate the characteristics of applying the traits in his own home towards his wife and children. Having the freedom to work on his abilities will show how available and present he'll be in spending quality time with you as the becoming woman.

We understand the importance of togetherness and the way it makes us feel; you know what I mean sis; that gentle kiss on the forehead, the holding of hands, the way he looks at you…come on now! But in all honesty, the becoming gentleman has to take time to build himself. Give him room and the respect to do so.

Despite past situations, when he is ready to open up about his past, respect it and gradually build from there. When you look back over your life and see how God was preparing the man and the woman in different forms, you'll thank God He didn't allow you to settle; the pain and tears were the testimony of unexpected breakthrough.

For this reason, we have to be careful in the way we speak about ourselves and others. Times are changing and God is in the business of transforming relationships for His Glory.

Seasons are shifting and the people who've been overlooked are now being chosen in a committed relationship leading to marriage. What joy this brings to my heart!

When it comes to Galatians 3:28, the Apostle Paul emphasises that there are neither Jew nor Gentiles, neither slave or free, nor is there male and female, for we are all one in Christ Jesus. In God's eyes, men and women are equal. This can also be applied in a relationship where both parties play a pivotal role in the home. For a couple to function successfully, there must be respect and honour where the becoming gentleman leads and the becoming woman follows.

The Becoming Woman

God doesn't want the becoming woman to squirm under the husband's leadership, but lean into the peace of mind that he gives. You can excel in your career, allow yourself to enjoy being nurtured, loved and protected by your husband, whilst being able to understand your husband's love and leadership in the home. This should not rob a woman of her strength, but simply keep both in balance by reconnecting with your softness and femininity.

A word of caution: To the becoming woman; if you are looking for a man to be your everything, remind yourself that God is the only One who already is your everything. God can and will work with the becoming gentleman, however, He will also work on you to know where your priorities are. When you expect perfection from the becoming gentleman, you are asking more than you can provide for yourself.

Let's look at God's plan: "She is your equal partner in God's gift of new life. Treat her as you should so your prayers will not be hindered." – 1 Peter 3:7. Women, if we submit to our husbands, our blessings won't be taken away and in turn make the role of the becoming gentleman easier. I am also aware that some men can be very abusive in certain relationships, so we must do our part to protect ourselves prior to making the commitment.

For this reason, some women haven't mastered the confidence or strength to be open and upfront to tell their partner how they feel. As a woman who is becoming the wife she intends to be, the becoming gentleman must learn to listen and understand her perspective to avoid manipulation and confusion. Yes, we have the right to vent in a mature manner, but not when it becomes detrimental and hurtful to both.

For the becoming gentleman to blossom effectively, he must give the woman space to express her thoughts and feelings to avoid keeping the hurt within her. A woman being in submission to her husband is not only honourable to him, but also honourable to God and allows peace to flow.

It is vitally important that as becoming women, we aren't constantly tangled in our emotions to solve problems on our own, rather, we learn how to build intimacy and trust in communicating effectively. When you encounter a difficult situation, remaining calm is very essential. In this case when they occur, take a few moments to breathe deeply whilst counting slowly to five.

The Becoming Woman

Looking after your physical health can improve your communication skills. As women, we shouldn't assume that our partners will always make us feel beautiful if we don't believe it for ourselves. We have to do the work underneath the surface and not be so dependent on a man's gentleness.

Being blindly in love without substance leads to an unstable foundation, and any negative thought harboured in your heart will interfere with parts of your brain used in language processing, listening and speech, as well as defensiveness and distrust.

The time will come where the man is able to talk about his upbringing in which the woman ought to be sensitive about how his family dynamics had an impact on the decisions made in the past, at present and for the future. This will help you be more understanding of whether this attitude will carry on or if he wants to start afresh with you.

As two unique individuals working on themselves daily, a positive trait which helps the physical and mental attributes is to smile. At times, we forget the power and beauty of smiling when plans don't go the way we expected. Pleasing memories and thoughts of people you care about creates opportunities to express kindness and compassion, stimulating trust and openness to others.

A gentle smile is a warm invite to being yourself. Maybe your husband is having a hard time at work. What if your smile could make his day? Even if it's by treating him or making his favourite food, it will be cherished.

Moving on, it is important to be mindful that men also have feelings and is seeking to work on them consistently for his aspiring wife to be. The becoming man understands the future and is working effortlessly to ensure you both enjoy quality bonding time and build for future generations. This is the purpose for the becoming gentleman because he has a vision and will pursue it.

When a man is committed to God, he will also be committed to you. A man after God's own heart will never lack any good thing!

The Becoming Woman

Remember that as you are maturing, so is the becoming gentleman. Learn to celebrate the work he's completed thus far and be expectant for what is yet to come. Being celebrated for the work that is accomplished changes the mood of the individual. It reminds them of their value and worth and how capable they are of soaring higher.

When you start using your words harshly over someone, they become more protective and in turn end up withdrawing. The acknowledgement of a man is essential and may not always be known, seen or discussed, but as a woman who is becoming, our words carry weight towards his wellbeing.

What we say to a gentleman who is becoming can uplift or bring him down. We are not taking this attitude into our futures ladies! You must ensure that what is spoken of starts with healthy thoughts and the ability to listen quickly. The becoming gentleman isn't forceful on how to get any woman; he is strategic and knows what he needs because the commitment to his purpose is evident in his pursuit.

The character of a man is determined by the woman he chooses, and as a becoming woman, we should learn how to develop healthy mental thought-patterns and become an asset to his progress. You may know of men who found a way to share his experiences in pursuing his wife and how he planned in advance what the future holds for him. When you encounter such men, remember they're still in the process to take the class of *becoming*.

How are you currently preparing yourself for the man God will bring your way?

_____

_____

_____

_____

_____

_____

The Becoming Woman

When getting to know my fiancé, it was a natural and organic approach. I knew God had a purpose to learn not only from him, but what my strengths and weaknesses were at the time. What I appreciate about my fiancé is his calm aura and wise ability on when to speak, the willingness to listen, learn and adapt in different environments, and making wise decisions that benefits the both of us. For this reason, I stand on this quote greatly:

> **When you can appreciate a man privately, he will celebrate you publicly!**

Men are important not only in a woman's life, but onto God, his family and friends. As a becoming woman, remember that when you celebrate and appreciate a man for how far he's come, the opportunities to enjoy the relationship will far exceed what you went through in the past.

Just like a becoming gentleman wants to feel and be loved by his aspiring wife, the woman must learn how to encourage, strengthen, celebrate and honour him. Who doesn't love surprises, especially if your love language is receiving gifts?!

To the becoming woman; be mindful of what comes out of your mouth and ensure you are speaking from a place of healing and not past wounds.

Reflection: The becoming gentleman is attracted to the woman who is on the journey to discovering herself. You need time to be who God intends, so pray, laugh, smile and be gentle towards each other. It's a process and despite the setbacks, you will both make it through! #*TheBecomingWoman*.

Chapter N.I.N.E.

-

Enjoy Your Life

"Live the life that's in front of you and embrace what is to come."

Whether you've been laid off from a lucrative job, in a lengthy relationship that didn't work out, recovering from a broken engagement, feeling vulnerable to love again or refusing to give men a chance; regardless of it all, learn to embrace and enjoy your life because it matters.

Your life is expensive; there will be moments where we may conclude that settling or not being sociable is the way forwards, especially to save ourselves from going through unexpected pain and trauma. Due to the intensity of situations, we tend to make permanent decisions mixed with emotional dysfunction that in the long run has an impact on our thought-patterns and how we see others. At times, we end up becoming comfortable with where we are and until we see change, we forfeit the beauty of what the current seasons are teaches us.

Have the following statements related to you at any point in your life?

- *"Until I get that full-time job with the lucrative salary, that's when I'll intentionally enjoy my life!"*
- *"Until I get married, have kids and buy a house, I'll be complete."*
- *"I am happy where I am; men can't be trusted and I refuse to be hurt again!"*
- *"External influences have made me vulnerable to love again."*
- *"What did I sign up for? I did not expect this breakup!"*

The Becoming Woman

No matter what situation you are in, you can still enjoy your life for what it is. You may not be where you want to be, but you have to realise that where you were isn't the place God intends for you to be forever. That's why He took you out of that relationship and allowed you to stay in the job you didn't like. He wants to develop your character with patience and humility.

It's very important to realise that where you are isn't permanent, but contributes greatly to the next level in your life. I am always amazed about the importance of enjoying my life whilst pursuing purpose, especially when I don't know the full picture. Rather than becoming agitated by what I don't yet know, I choose to focus on building current assets, my knowledge and the ability to keep going. Our world is vast and waiting for answers, solutions and encouragement to persevere.

I don't believe in covering up pain as that can lead to unhealthy pride, however, I do believe that honouring the struggles will help to appreciate the journey. I remember talking to a friend about the beauty of the unknown and how we ought to prepare for what we can't yet see. When obstacles come your way, it's easy to neglect them and pretend they don't exist, but at some stage in our lives, we'll end up misusing others and making it the norm.

From a relationship perspective, working on your peace whilst enjoying each other's company is essential and those around you will find the courage to believe they too can have healthy relationships. Waiting patiently for the man God has prepared for you is already set in motion. You have to be disciplined to constantly seek God as your first source of strength because distractions are real and can take place at any time, especially in the waiting season.

If you keep fighting your current season without having a clear understanding that God could be using that period to build you up, you'll end up taking short cuts and starting over. I know about the pressure of patience and waiting for your heart's desires to fall in place, but what could that moment in your life be teaching you personally? In effect, what attitude will you carry around because you're fed up of waiting?

A confident individual who enjoys their life doesn't carry around negative thoughts, neither do they entertain the mindset of stagnation. Enjoying your life is being able to cherish and appreciate what you already have with the expectation that what you believe is coming will arrive when the time is ready. Enjoying your life means to endure the beauty of waiting whilst standing strong.

A famous quote from Bishop TD Jakes says: "Can you stand to be blessed?" In other words, can you cope with the level of blessing that is coming your way? Are you prepared for the responsibility and weight the blessings carry? We see the opportunity and assume we are ready. Ladies, it's okay to not be ready. You don't need to force what isn't yours and can enjoy life from the inside out. It can be tough because pressure provokes pride as some people can't always cope or handle constructive criticism, but that is how you learn to grow and mature. It's easy to focus on what you want to hear which isn't always healthy for your mental wellbeing.

Proverbs 27:6 says that 'hurtful words from a friend are better than kisses from an enemy.' What am I saying? Proverbs refers to having a true friend/confidant who will lovingly tell you what you need to change about your life to save a lot of pain in the future.

What we don't always recognise are blind spots, and at times we either miss or overlook them as non-essential, but anything blurry ends up being difficult to solve, especially when the root of the matter hasn't been identified.

We all have blind spots, and it's those areas which cause us to ignore the healing process. What you don't resolve at the early stages will end up following you, and this also applies in building relationships and connections with others. To enjoy your life is to speak truthfully to a loved one and help the person with their own journey. You ought to *be* the change, allowing it to reflect towards others. Life will constantly evolve, but we have the responsibility to not be triggered by it, rather, we can grow and become better to love what's exposed of us.

Enjoying your life doesn't mean you need have it all together.

At one moment in my life, I remember speaking to God about being a 'broken vessel.' As the becoming woman evolves into who she is called to be, it will require honesty to understand that she has cracks in her life which needs to be worked on and can't be done alone. Through the power of the Holy Spirit, He has the capacity to fill her up if she lets Him in. What you can't do on your own will be multiplied through His intervention and you know it's going to be a very good job well done! There's a time and season for everything, however, what you can achieve and fulfil is better than procrastinating about it and waiting for the perfect timing. If you don't have the vision to see your life from a growth perspective, the vision becomes blurry because how you see yourself is a reflection of how your life will be.

I am not saying that we should force knowing what our lives should be or look like, but with each step, we learn, ask relevant questions and are optimistic as it makes the journey pleasant and enjoyable. Following on from this, when we are waiting for breakthroughs and answers, we must ensure that our thoughts aren't entertaining the following points:

- **Anger** – When used correctly, constructive anger builds, but when used incorrectly, it passively crushes especially when you haven't taken the opportunity to release your hurts in a healthy manner. When you vent your pain towards those around you, it doesn't only impact you internally, but your environments and those around you who sense your presence. Enjoying life is about managing your emotions in a healthy manner and freely talking about them as a way of release.

- **Resentment** – This is a big topic that needs to be addressed wisely. The becoming woman has no time to entertain any form of resentment or offence, neither being offended by others regardless of what the situation is. In our own strength, it will never be easy, but we can choose to shift our focus towards forgiveness and let go rather than harbouring bitterness towards ourselves and others.

- **Pride** – What you refuse to confess or admit will eventually lead to false humility and pride. When you are able to admit areas in your life that aren't aligning up to what you expected, pride will create a fabricated perception of

The Becoming Woman

freedom, assuming you don't need to open up and be whole. This leads to more pride growing. Don't pretend to be fine for fear of being judged by others; you would be very surprised that what someone else is struggling in is what you're also struggling with too. Be real, and once you are open about it, move on and enjoy the life God has given you.

- **Hurt** – The constant repetition of what happened in the past including the guilt which comes with it can cause you to hurt yourself in many ways. There is a saying that goes: 'Hurt People, Hurt People.' When we are hurt by someone especially when there's no maturity/discernment in the friendship or relationship, we are eager to hurt them back. We haven't found the true remedy of learning how to cast our anxieties, rather, we choose to add pressure and carry the weight of the hurt which impacts those around us. Enjoying your life is about leaving the hurts behind and being the best version of yourself.

- **Low Self-Esteem** – Why is this such a battle for the becoming woman? Due to unreliable emotions, you attract negative thoughts especially when unexpected news or patterns of the past occurs. No matter who you are, sis, YOU ARE ENOUGH! You are responsible for improving your growth and breaking free from comfort zones. You have the power of Christ to enjoy every moment of your life regardless of how it looks to the external. Pick yourself up and don't you dare belittle the beautiful woman you are becoming.

- **Dominant Mindset** – In the single season, you have the freedom to do what you believe is best for your wellbeing, however, you are also responsible for your mindset, your lifestyle, where you go, who you meet etc. As the becoming woman, you must analyse the thoughts of dominance which can come from family patterns, a close friend or someone you may be interested in knowing. As mentioned previously in this chapter regarding blind spots, it's very important that we are aware of aggressive habits or impatience that our

The Becoming Woman

thoughts bring when we overlook and assume we are ready for the relationship. When your heart is bitter, it's more likely to be defensive and this behavioural pattern robs you of enjoying life in its entirety, therefore, monitor your thoughts in temporal seasons of testing.

All the above is what we should avoid when enjoying each season in our lives. Those who don't know how to enjoy their life end up carrying these toxic characteristics into their relationships, friendships and even family members. This should not be the case, and for those struggling with being single, those years will pay off when you look over your life and see real transformation evolve, remembering that challenges aren't permanent; it's just not ready to be released yet. A blessing released too soon is not a blessing at all and yes, it may be painful, but you will embrace it with time.

On the other hand, we must learn to understand that enjoying your life doesn't mean there won't be mountains and battles to overcome. Instead, you can make the most of each season by embracing what there is to learn from them. As an optimistic woman who is always open to learning, I accept the fact that not knowing everything in life is for my good. For this reason, it makes me more aware of why God doesn't always give us the full picture and narrows our focus to depend on Him.

> "Nobody told me the road would be easy, and I don't believe He's brought me this far to leave me!"
>
> Mary Mary – Can't Give Up Now.

There will be tears and you will fail at some point but because God gives us life daily, we can be assured that He will help us get through our problems. There are two rules to remember when enjoying seasons of change:

Rule number 1: Never give up on life! I know it's not always easy, but you must understand that your journey is for His Glory.

The Becoming Woman

Sometimes, it seems confusing why God is silent, but what we may not always realise is that His silence doesn't equate to His absence. Having faith is believing in what we can't see in the physical but knowing it's already manifested in accordance to His Will. You don't always need to talk or know about what is happening. Being still and believing is what's essential to keep going.

Rule number 2: Our pain serves a high purpose! We don't go through pain in vain but to serve someone else going through a similar situation. God will never leave you so enjoy where you are because seasons are changing. Sorrow may come in the evening, but joy comes in the morning! You will be surprised when what used to hurt you is the tool which ignites others around you to overcome their own hurts. I enjoy being able to share my joys and vulnerable moments because together, they create greater strength and tenacity to keep going.

When travelling with my fiancé for his birthday, I posted a video on my story about our trip and a friend replied to it and said "You give me the strength to believe in love again." I didn't have to ask her to elaborate because I understood what she was referring to.

As women, we understand our language, and all I could do was remind her that God will provide the companion at the appointed time and heal broken hearts. When we've been hurt, especially by someone we thought would stay, it's easy to neglect the beauty of love but when you realise it didn't break you, you build stamina and the ability to open up to others.

> **I believe that heartbreak shouldn't impact or deter you from believing God for your partner. We must be mindful to sympathise with our loved ones but not allow it to affect our perception of love towards others.**

As a woman in her single season, maximise the beauty of exploring and traveling as a way of learning and opening up to new environments. It's easy to focus on being with a man and travelling

The Becoming Woman

with him, however, I challenge you to step out boldly and embrace solo trips. Choose a beautiful destination and make an intentional decision to go there and embrace change.

There will always be key gems to take away because what you aren't exposed to in your comfort zone will be revealed in another situation. What we take for granted is what others are believing for. We are able to learn from others including their walks of life, what they currently do and how to add value into their lives. Expansion and trust are built when we provide something greater than ourselves rather than focusing on what we can gain.

> **Take each day at a time and embrace what's already in your reach!**

We learn by example, observation and experience. We live in a world which is constantly changing and becoming easily influenced by impatience. When the tempting seasons of cutting corners feels more attractive, you will remember that where you are going in life is determined by what you learn in the present moment and how you're able to pass the season. Your destiny depends on your personal discipline and where you're placing your focus on.

Let this short chapter remind you to enjoy every moment of your life unapologetically and create amazing memories with your loved ones. Cherish each day to live on purpose because life is a gift. Your wellbeing is vital so ensure you are intentionally present to consume every joy that comes within. You are not a mistake and all you've been through isn't in vain. The difficult moments won't always go away, but it will never outlast the seasons of on-going enjoyment.

Ultimately, remember that your relationship with Jesus is the top priority no matter where you are in life. When you invest in a relationship with your First Love, you will realise that He alone is enough for you, and will reveal the ways you can grow step by step. Don't put your life on hold because you aren't with a man. God is able to provide someone who will add value to your life. Although a man is the protector, he won't be a replacement for your relationship with God.

The Becoming Woman

ENJOY YOUR LIFE! Cherish and steward everything you've been given because it will be accounted for. Appreciate the journey and pursue healthy ambitions. Let's forgive ourselves for the pain endured and release it. You have everything to enjoy the different stages of life. To grasp the beauty of the journey is to enjoy each day with its unique challenges. We are able to use the lessons to advance the present and future endeavours when transitioning from the season of singleness to courting.

So, I say once again; enjoy your life and all it has to offer. Your time to be found is in motion.

Dear Becoming Woman; where you are is not a mistake. God chose you to be where you are and with His leading, you are safe. Enjoy your life because you WILL achieve great accomplishments! *#TheBecomingWoman*.

Chapter T.E.N.

-

Own Your Season

"The beauty of owning your season is in the key lessons learnt along the way. What you embrace is what you are able to change and transition into new levels of growth."

No matter where you are, always remember that times and seasons will always change. We have nearly come to the end of the book. What have you taken away from it? To own your season is to remember that you are accepted in the Beloved. When it seems as if nothing is happening in your life, remember that a book isn't written and published in a day; each page takes you on a journey of discovery leading you to know more.

When you enjoy your own company without trying to put on a façade, you start to accept where you are and expect great change in due course. It is important to pass the current season you're in and focus on building yourself up one step at a time. When you embrace the present season including being single, you are able to trust that God has tomorrow in His Hands. After all, tomorrow belongs to God as Matthew 6:34 puts it.

We ought to see every season as opportunities to embrace what's in front of us. Being in the single season enables us to seek God intimately, understanding the purpose He has for us to fulfil. The greatest moments are when you embrace singleness with the key ingredient of patience and allow God to fulfil your utmost desires.

You learn how to own your season when you ask God to reveal His purpose, and I believe when you carry out His tasks, what you are believing for will come at the appointed time.

Your obedience to carry out that purpose effectively is linked to owning every part of the journey without taking shortcuts and being open minded to what is around you. There is great beauty in seasons of pain – the pain of waiting or feeling you are left behind as it builds stamina and inner-strength to be bold and work on the broken places in your life.

The Becoming Woman

At times, you may feel looked down on by others because of your status and it's easy to start believing you are left behind because each season looks the same.

I remember speaking with my sister about current seasons and how our perspectives change on where we are, where we are going, and what we should expect without forcing anything to happen by learning to enjoy the present moment. When you are so focused on what hasn't yet happened, it can block what is coming your way, because whatever is revealed too soon may be mishandled. You can't focus on fixing everything at once without learning how to enjoy what the current season is teaching you.

> **As the becoming woman seeks to be in a relationship, she must learn how to work on herself by loving the season she's in rather than having thoughts of being elsewhere.**

We need to be mindful of our thoughts which leads to different perceptions that either increase our development or make us start again. No matter what thoughts are going through your mind, you belong to God and He understands the season you are in. He placed you in the current season to be a pillar of strength for those who are facing challenges, so you can be His mouthpiece to bring peace and comfort to others.

Your life is numbered and as the writer of Luke 12:7 reminds us that because God knows the number of hairs on our head, how much more will He not graciously desire to change our seasons at the appointed time. In seasons of transition, it will test your faith, but remember that when your faith is activated, it enables you to pursue the good fight of perseverance.

God moves with joy when you trust Him and unswervingly hold onto His promises because they are ready to be released in due season. Don't look back but forwards because that is where your divine breakthrough is – the single season will eventually turn into fruitful and Godly relationships leading to marriage to carry out His ultimate purpose.

The Becoming Woman

Storytime: I visited bridal stores and made bookings to try on a few wedding dresses in the summer period of 2019 with two dear friends. What inspired me to do this was my travel back to the UK from Valencia. My girls stood with me throughout the duration and was a pleasant and unique experience I'll never forget.

Following on this, my beautiful sister also took time out to visit wedding shops and tried on bridal dresses in the summer period of 2021. For what I could not yet see happen at the time of being single, I declared that at the appointed time, I will be wearing my own wedding dress.

You know it's real when you look at the photos and see the transformation, from speaking it into existence and seeing it in reality. I encourage you to make an enquiry about a wedding store, book in an appointment and try on different bridal dresses for inspiration and creating memories. This is the preparation stages of faith and the promises spoken over your life being manifested.

The beauty of life is to understand our seasons and how they're working for our good, for we know that delays prepare the testimonies. We can't be ignorant that there is such pressure in our society to be married at a certain age and have children, however, I want to encourage you to be still.

In Romans 5:3-5 (NIV) Apostle Paul reminds us that when we go through various seasons of testing, it enables us to persevere which builds our character and hope. Being single is an opportunity to learn from quality married couples who've been through the ups and downs of life, yet keeps going.

I encourage the upcoming generation to invest and study books which focus on embracing singleness, wholeness, and being intentional about healthy partnerships between you and your spouse before saying 'I do.' Surround yourself with healthy married couples and don't be afraid to ask questions at the relevant times.

The single season is the opportunity to embrace your unique journey. To rush into a season of being in a relationship, particularly if there are unhealed wounds from the past will eventually come up in future relationships towards others. Knowing you've healed from those who've hurt you and those you've also hurt are gradual steps that will indicate a healthy committed relationship between each other.

The Becoming Woman

God knows the right time to give you a spouse and this starts with being honest with your struggles. Your greatest gift is letting go and reminding yourself of God's unfailing promises. No matter how unseen you feel right now, it is for a season. In these moments, we should be bold to believe that new beginnings are emerging and seasons of delay will always birth a greater outcome.

> **God never forgets those who He hides for a season!**

The greater the waiting period, the greater the blessing. It may seem that the waiting season is punishment, but wouldn't it be better to wait well and enjoy the relationship than rush without seeing the vision ahead? As I started to appreciate and cherish the single season, I came across the number 7 which represents completion. Having been in the season of intentionally waiting, it encouraged me to invest in other women and remind them of their worth to make every moment count and be thankful for what they have.

Owning your season opens your mind to the intentionality of God and not take His Presence for granted. Because He is the matchmaker of your life, take the time to be present with what He is doing because we know how much He loves and wants the best for us.

As becoming women, we should distinguish when it's time to be around others and privately seek Him. In the courting stages, you will find moments where you miss being alone with God and this isn't to say that it won't continue because you're now in a relationship. Your intentions to know God are dependent on how willing you are to create time for Him as your first priority.

Seasons are beautiful when we learn to embrace them from a fresh perspective. When I look back over the years of waiting and considering what my life would look like once I become one with my spouse was the same investment I applied to work on myself internally; *Note*: this is an on-going process.

I used my season of singleness to help aspiring authors in storytelling and book writing, hosting various workshops virtually and in-person, being an advocate for authors, business owners and

The Becoming Woman

their stories. I knew there was far more in me than waiting until my prayers were answered. I was confident that God will answer, and He did and still is!

Servitude is extremely powerful and should be our mantle each day. When you are true about what you provide, the right people will invest in what you do. Positioning yourself in the right community is about purpose to help others in their endeavours. You'll know where you fit in the community and eventually build genuine relationships with others as a way to encourage them to own their season and maximise life to its fullest capacity.

> **I didn't entertain discontentment without taking the time to understand what the season was teaching me. There is a time to celebrate and a time to be still. Both seasons are beautiful in their own way.**

Although tough times are present, they will not last forever. Sister; your season is changing each moment and so is your heart. Yes, you will be frustrated at times, but your season teaches you to respond in a calm manner so you're able to listen first before giving a response.

As we continue our individual seasons, the attention becomes more on how to please God, trusting that He knows every need for companionship whilst drawing intimately closer to Him.

April 2020 was a life changing season. At the early peaks of the Coronavirus, I sat in the living room whilst listening to the news. At the time, I reflected on life and the severe impact the disease of Covid-19 had on all of us locally and globally. I'd thought of ways to add further value in the community through recording encouraging videos on YouTube whilst pivoting with Authentic Worth Publishing's services as I'd discovered how to navigate and find useful strategies for its ongoing success in storytelling.

I read a devotional about the beauty of gifts and remember feeling so empowered to do more with them. A video I have on my YouTube channel currently is called 'Stop sitting on your gifts' and it continues to inspire and remind me about my purpose. At that time, my focus wasn't on being in a relationship but wanting to help aspiring authors publish their stories and meet other like-minded people virtually.

Being a woman of contentment was about the solutions I was able to provide in the community and not being distracted from my desires. In the waiting season, there are opportunities to nurture our gifts whilst pursuing purpose. Being in a relationship and being single are uniquely important. Let's not create a false or negative perception of being with a man the main goal and disregard the beauty of owning the season of singleness.

Creating quality time with your friends and family is a massive contribution to our mental and emotional wellbeing. Be mindful that singleness doesn't equate to loneliness and using the opportunity to develop yourself should be your priority so the man looking for you knows what he is pursuing.

Although the aim of this book is to encourage and prepare **The Becoming Woman** for the transformation of singleness to courting, it is birthed from an internal decision of how content you are in being single whilst spending quality time with yourself to understand who you are.

We shouldn't assume that being in a relationship will fix or take away our problems. No matter what we try to hide, if we don't confront those situations in a healthy manner, it will cause delay and tension. We must be mindful to allow love to work naturally in our hearts so that everything we desire will happen at the right time.

In your single season:

- Pray in tongues regularly and with trusted friends
- Fast regularly
- Study and meditate on the Word daily
- Take your physical health seriously
- Don't keep looking back and wanting your old life
- Open your heart to embrace what's ahead of you
- Be prepared to serve in your church or local community centre

The Becoming Woman

Anything impactful takes time and isn't to be rushed. What's important is being in alignment with what God says. Looking back over my journey, I overcame the distractions and pressures to settle and trusted what God promised me. Now it has come to pass! The wait was worth it, and during my single season, I chose peace to accept each day in both the good and difficult moments.

I encourage you, Becoming Woman not to remain complacent but find your purpose and give value to your community. Don't wait until the man you desire comes. In the meantime, embrace who you are becoming. Audit your time and make sure you focus on what matters most.

You don't need approval or affirmation from your environments; all you need is to embrace what each day brings and find ways to enhance your life and transition gracefully into the season of courting by cherishing every moment the single season is teaching you.

Dear Becoming Woman: When you see why God made you wait, you'll learn to appreciate the journey ahead of you. Though you cry and feel that time isn't on your side, take what the single process is teaching you with great intention. Respect yourself by covering your peace, your mind and your body. Above all, own your season and what it's currently teaching you! #*TheBecomingWoman*.

10 Truths The Becoming Woman Needs to Know

Alongside the purpose of The Becoming Woman, I want to leave you with 10 truths to encourage your journey of singleness to courting. Remember that what is for you will not pass you by; despite it feeling like a slow process, it will turn out for your good:

Truth 1 – Remember who your Initial First Love is
Truth 2 – When it's Difficult to Pray
Truth 3 – Owning your Season
Truth 4 – Rest in My Love
Truth 5 – I created Love
Truth 6 – Remember your Crown
Truth 7 – The Art of Gratitude
Truth 8 – Be Intimate with Me
Truth 9 – Patience in the Waiting Season
Truth 10 – Trust the Process

Truth 1 – Remember who your Initial First Love is
When you wake up in the morning, what's the first thought on your mind? It's easy to focus on planning the day ahead without acknowledging the One who gives life and guidance. He expresses unfailing love each morning through nature. Let this be a reminder of how valuable and precious you are. His love has been permanently purchased for your existence. Cherish it well.

Truth 2 – When it's Difficult to Pray
In vulnerable and testing moments, words are difficult to articulate or express especially when all you see is answered prayers for others but yourself. You wonder what's happening, however, when you least expect it, the still, gentle voice speaks and says 'I am with you through it all!' This reminds us that the Holy Spirit intercedes with words that are few, yet so powerful that even shedding a tear can change your life. He emphasises again; 'I will never leave you nor forsake you.' Prayer is what keeps you going on the journey and

believing for what is yet to come. It is your weapon against mental illness and a giving up attitude.

Truth 3 – Owning your Season
When you own your season, no one can use it against you. When you are confident in your singleness, you are more patient, intentional and influential towards those who are in the waiting season. You focus on purpose because you remember seasons always change, and though you may be hidden, you will eventually be found. Be mindful not to entertain quick-fixes. The writer of Ecclesiastes 3:11 says that God makes **all** things beautiful in His time. This scripture encourages us to own the seasons we are in, for at the appointed time, we will see every desire come into fruition. Delay is not denial so don't despise where you are. Instead, be open-minded and seek guidance on what you can learn from each day and continue the journey.

Truth 4 – Rest in My Love
Before someone takes My position in your heart, remember that I am the Vine. In order for Me to provide abundant blessings for you, ponder on My unfailing love; for I am a Good, Good Father who knows what you need at the right time. Take rest in Me and watch how I turn your life around for good. It may seem undaunting now because it feels you've been waiting for so long, but I know when you are ready to handle the blessing you desire. I don't want to give it to you prematurely. Rest in my love first and allow me to lead you in safety to the ordained spouse that is created for you. Be still!
#selah

Truth 5 – I created Love
I am love because I created it. I know the power of love between two people; it's like a Father-Son bond. They are stronger together than apart. Before I reveal your partner, walk in My stable love. I will teach you how a Godly spouse should love and nurture you. Trust me; the Creator, Author and Finisher of love. My nature is love; that is what I am to you.

Truth 6 – Remember your Crown
Remember how valuable you are; you are prized treasure which can't be compromised. You are more than pearls and rubies. Because of how precious, valuable and expensive you are, I've hidden you for a season and will release your crown when it's the right time. Instead, bask and enjoy the present moment with Me. You don't need to belittle or lower your standards for anyone. I want you to be whole in who you are and what you've been called to be.

Truth 7 – The Art of Gratitude
I love when you remember how good I've been to you. I enjoy when you write down all the great blessings in your journal to remind you of My Faithfulness. It represents maturity and a heart of expectations. I will give what you didn't ask for because your heart is filled with so much gratitude. The more grateful you are for the waiting seasons, the better you'll become when choosing to grow in the grace of thankfulness. Your gratitude makes it easy for me to move in ways you wouldn't expect. Remember the Great I Am whilst being thankful because this is a lifestyle which impacts you in every season.

Truth 8 – Be Intimate with Me
My love for you is intimate; when your mind wanders off, I am still present with you. I watch each day and desire for you to spend quality time with Me. When you remember how intimate I desire to be with you, it puts everything into perspective. Abide in Me and I will abide in you. When you do so, the fruits in your life will speak for itself. Don't forget that I am always jealous about you. When you come to Me with everything, it becomes easier to manage. You become creative when you draw close to me and prepare yourself for what I have in store.

Truth 9 – Patience in the Waiting Season
Actively position your mind to be patient because the greatest blessings are reserved for those who walk confidently in God even when they don't have their desires met. My love requires you to wait and keep your focus on Me. I will give you peace whilst you wait for My best. Being still is a form of faith in the waiting season. When

patience is being activated, it's because I am preparing and creating the moments you've been waiting for.

Truth 10 – Trust the Process
Each day requires you to trust Me. When you truly acknowledge Me for who I am and not only for what you can gain, your paths will be perfectly directed. Don't lean on how you feel because emotions can't be trusted, but My Word which never fails can be trusted. Remember the process is teaching you more than you'll expect, so take the time to understand what each step reveals along the journey and cherish it in your heart.

The Becoming Woman

We are now at the end of the book! How did you find it and what were your key takeaways?

_____

_____

_____

_____

_____

_____

Sharing experiences of my journey with you has been a pleasant yet humbling opportunity. It is with great pleasure that this book isn't just read and kept away, but use it as a guide when you are off track or wanting to give up on love and life.

Remember no matter what you are facing right now, you are a masterpiece in the making. Cherish every season and stage in your life because what didn't happen in the past will come to fruition in the future.

If God did it before, He will do it again!

I'll leave you with the chorus from a song called ***"Do It Again"*** by Elevation Worship:

Your Promise still stands
Great is Your faithfulness, faithfulness
I'm still in Your hands
This is my Confidence
You've never failed me yet
Never failed me yet.

Becoming Woman; you are evolving in the making!

Thank you for reading The Becoming Woman to reflect, ponder and invest in the <u>better</u> version of yourself. We'd appreciate if you could leave a review on the website: www.authenticworth.com/books and other online book retailers.

This book is dedicated to women locally and globally who are changing lives one step at a time through storytelling, inspiration, influence and legacy.

Your time awaits you – be positioned because change has already started.

Recommended books for the woman on her journey:

- It's Time to Heal – A Woman's Journey to Self-Discovery and Freedom
- Confident Face – Embracing your Authentic Beauty

Other books written by the author:

- Completion – From the Perspective of Brokenness
- From Glory to Glory – Great Beauty in Seasons of Pain; Strong at the Broken Places
- The Power of a Forward-Thinking Mindset – Breaking Strongholds in the Mind
- Abundant Progress – Maximising the Gradual Steps of the Journey

All books are on the website: www.authenticworth.com/books

Notes

Notes

Notes

Notes

www.ingramcontent.com/pod-product-compliance
Lightning Source LLC
Chambersburg PA
CBHW022043160426
43209CB00002B/54